AFRICAN SPIRITUALITY:

(*An Anthology of Igbo Religious Myths*)

Collected and interpreted by

Udobata R Onunwa

(Revised and Enlarged edition)

Published 2005 by arima publishing

www.arimapublishing.com

ISBN 1-84549-057-6

Printed and bound in the United Kingdom

Typeset in Garamond 11/14

arima publishing
ASK House, Northgate Avenue
Bury St Edmunds, Suffolk IP32 6BB
t: (+44) 01284 700321

www.arimapublishing.com

Dedication
To the wise elders and custodians of
African Traditional Religion and Culture

Foreword
By Professor Edmund C. O. Ilogu

In retirement, I look back to many research projects, which I could not complete. The thought makes me feel I did not leave enough legacies for younger scholars to inherit. However, this feeling is fulfilled whenever any of my former students comes up with what I could have done myself. I pick up courage and move on trusting that I have not laboured in vain. It gives me a feeling of joy and pride to see some materials published for wider circulation. I am glad to say that I groomed many articulate and brilliant minds who are now '*mightier than I*"

I am pleased to see the completion of the *African Spirituality: An Anthology of Igbo Religious Myths* by Professor Udobata Onunwa. He was one of the best students I taught and supervised during my long university career at the University of Nigeria. He has been a prolific writer and I feel pleased to be asked to write a preface to this book. He chose me to do this not only because I was his teacher but also I had wanted to work with him on a number of research projects and particularly the one that produced this book, but for the problem of time! My commitments in the public service at the Federal and State Government Services of Nigeria, the wider world of academia and the Church, have not allowed me any time to embark on serious research work in recent years.

This is the first comprehensive work on Igbo Myths by an indigenous Igbo scholar. The strength of the book lies in the numerous resources at the author's disposal, which he effectively and appropriately utilised. He is an articulate and creative writer, a resourceful and diligent researcher, an able teacher and an expert in African Traditional Institutions and Culture. He is also an Igbo by extraction, versed in the rich heritage of his people's culture and traditions. He is no stranger to the very people whose myths, religious worldview and philosophy he has collected and analysed in this book. The work, therefore, has an academic merit and market potential. It is important to remark that this book will undoubtedly make an enormous contribution to the growing discipline of African Studies in general and the on-going quest into various aspects of Igbo thought and life.

The author's main aim for this work is academic, having known him as a university teacher. I see beyond that. The book is going to be an invaluable tool in the hands of policy-makers and administrators in Africa. European scholars and business entrepreneurs as well as administrative officers who want to understand and interpret African ways of life and thought purely for enhancing international relationships and business enterprises will find the book a very helpful guide and rich mine of wisdom. Besides, general readers will enjoy the humorous tales and picturesque literary image of African life simply and graphically presented. Although the ancestors of the Africans and particularly the Igbo did not document their wisdom in any literary form, they were, nonetheless, intellectual giants in their own rights. The ability of the author to retrieve this fast disappearing rich mine of knowledge is a very important and worthwhile investment for which Africa in general and Igbo society in particular would be grateful. The culture area from which the myths were collected is wide enough to be described as representing the entire African World. The use of Culture-Area Approach is a new dimension in research methodology in social sciences.

I, therefore, commend this book to the wider readership it deserves- to students, teachers, policy-makers, international diplomats, church dignitaries, business executives and everyone genuinely interested and involved in development of Africa.

Edmund C. O. Ilogu
Retired Professor and Dean
Faculty of Social Sciences, University of Nigeria Nsukka
And Commissioner, Public Complaints Commission
Enugu, Nigeria

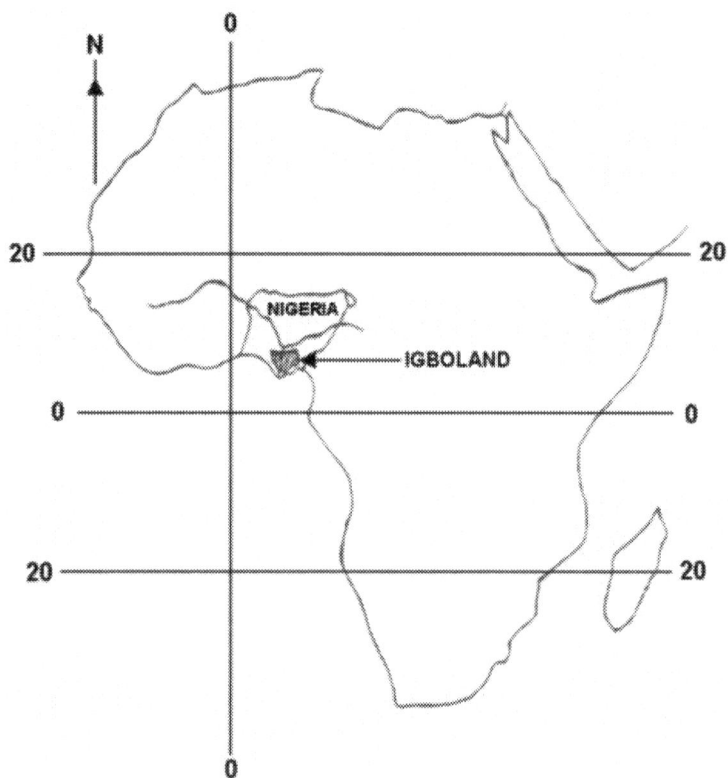

MAP OF AFRIKA SHOWING THE LOCATION OF NIGERIA AND IGBOLAND

TABLE OF CONTENTS

Introduction

To attempt to penetrate the extremely complex domain of African spirituality is a task that needs personal contact with the living votaries and practitioners of the traditional religion and culture. Such existential and participatory study of the Traditional African Religion and Culture would certainly be involving and exerting in its demands of intellectual resources, time, patience and objectivity. Much has been done at the descriptive level by a good number of detached and armchair scholars. An in-depth and analytical study is what people need in this 21st Century. This does not mean that people had not previously done any interpretative work on the religion. However Western scholars and some indigenous Africans who attempted to interpret the traditional religion and culture of Africa did so with Western theological and philosophical concepts, often alien to the votaries of the religion. The late Ugandan scholar, Okot P'Bitek reacted in the early 1970's against what he described as *dressing the African deities in Hellenic Western garb* (P'Bitek, 1970,p. 47) African studies have been seriously handicapped by this type of hermeneutical problem.

Attempts to *understand* African Traditional Religion has been an on-going phenomenon. Writing several years ago, Walter Freytag warned his fellow European writers that studying African Religion and culture

> *is much more than providing information. It is trying to understand.*
> *There is a great difference between them. The mere possession of*
> *information may involve no change at all. But understanding involves*
> *a two-way traffic. For you do not understand until you have been*
> *touched (affected) yourself, until you get a new insight into who you are*
> *yourself. In the study of other religions, you can amass information*

about their scripture and doctrine. But you have not understood them until you have been compelled to interpret your own...

(Freytag quoted by Warren, 1959, p. 164).

This line of thought challenged Marcel Griaule to attempt in the mid 1940s to understand the religion of the Dogon of Mali in the West African sub region. He did, as it were, a stimulating study of the people and discovered for himself what he described as the Dogon world-view. Through a period of thirty-three successive days of serious conversation and discussion with Ogotemmeli, a veritable and knowledgeable old priest, Griaule discovered the *under- girding cosmology behind African beliefs and actions.* (Griaule, 1965 p. 2) He thus came out with the conclusion that African religious systems are not merely a reflection of the socio economic systems but autonomous and systemic spheres of thought and action.

Africans are known to speak on many occasions in oblique allusions and proverbs. This has in several ways confounded the Western interpreters whose way of thought is quite different. The Igbo of South Eastern Nigeria, for instance, are fond of adapting their thought to basic obvious forms of expressions when dealing with people of other ethnic groups and races. That is why a literal interpretation or understanding of the statements of a traditional Igbo sage does not fully express his thoughts and ideas.

We shall attempt to peer into the Igbo world through the analysis of one kind of those oblique allusions and verbal symbols by which they express their thought. In this analysis, we shall try to bring the two worlds (spiritual and physical) together symbolically. In trying to understand this vision of reality, one must realise that there is an obvious fact of entering a different world of strange and unusual perspectives and relationships. Until one realises this fact, one may not truly understand the real meaning of a particular religious system or worldview. It is difficult to comprehend a system from a detached standpoint.

In an attempt to probe into the world of a different culture and religion, one may come into contact with symbols that may often dismay or repel. Such symbols may be either verbal or physical. The verbal symbols are in oral literature, songs, poetry and tales of different kinds. Since many traditional Africans did not learn the art of writing in time, they communicated their ideas by oral symbolism.

One of the earliest writings discovered in the African continent was the Egyptian Hieroglyphics- or Picture Writing, which did not spread far down South of Sahara. Around the 18th century AD, it was discovered that another form of writing called **Nsibidi** had been in use along the coast of the West African sub-region. It was popular among some members of Secret Societies like **Ekpe** and among the rich middle class elites. It was not common among the peasants and therefore did not take long before it faded into oblivion and its extant forms are hard to reproduce.

The Language of Art was another form of writing known in many parts of the tropical African continent. This served as the interpretative model and means of expression of different forms of ideas. Religious art was more common than others. Carving or sculpture also served as a means of communication of ideas and invariably became the scripture of many religious beliefs.

Religious artefacts predominated and suffused everywhere. No wonder the Early European visitors to Africa daubed African traditional religion *idolatry;* for the visible icons were the main thing they saw.

The Oral Symbol, which we have chosen to analyse in this book, is the Myth. A fundamental question, which comes to mind in this study, is the meaning and function of myths in people's life. A general understanding of what they are and do may then lead us to an in-depth explanation and interpretation of what we might identify as myths in Igbo traditional religion and culture.

Simply put, one may say that myths in Igbo society are stories about gods. (Childs, 1960: p. 9). They usually directly or indirectly exist in narrative form and prose. The Igbo, like other Africans, think in mythical terms. In general term, Nicholas Berdyaer has stated *that:*

> *myth is a reality , immeasurably greater than concept…It is high time we stopped looking at myth with invention, with the illusions of primitive mentality, and with anything, in fact, which is essentially opposed to reality…Myth is always concrete and expresses life better than abstract thought can do; its nature is bound up with that of a symbol. Myth is the concrete recital of events and original phenomena of the spiritual life symbolised in the rational world, which has engraved itself on the language, memory and creative energy of the people….*

(Berdyaer, 1935, p. 70)

Some other scholars have given various definitions and explanations of myth. According to Geoffrey Parrinder,

> *myth is a story of unhistorical or supernatural beings, as distinct from a legend, which refers to a historical person. Myths are found in all religions and culture and are taken as statements of fact… A symbolical representation is meant to indicate a reality, which is essentially beyond description.*

(Parrinder, 1971, p. 196)

The Encyclopaedia Americana defines it as

> *stories told as symbols of fundamental truths within societies having a strong oral traditions*

(Encyclopaedia Americana, 1987, p. 699)

Yet writing over a generation ago, Carl Gustav Jung saw myths *not as indices of or a charter for cultural institutions but as psychological realities, expressions of archetypes or primordial images of the collective unconscious.*

(Jung (ed.) Jacobi, 1961 p. 314)

Benjamin Ray and J. Vansina have in the more recent past added a few ideas that seem current in the academic analysis of mythical saga. According to Professor Ray,

a myth is a history of sacred events presented in a way to explain the world as it is.

(Ray, 1976, p. 91)

This is a very crucial point in the sense that Ray has taken a stand to validate the claims that oral and non-documented evidence can be taken seriously as history in its own right. So oral history can be used as a valid evidence to reconstruct events unlike many historiographers who castigated the use of oral data as a valid evidence to reconstruct African past.

J. Vansina states that:

account that originate out of speculation by local sagas…Mythical accounts justify the bases of existing society and correspond to a timeless past. Myths seem to be accounts of origin believed by the tellers to be true but held by outsiders to be fiction.

(Vansina, 1985 p. 6)

Herman Baumann in his pioneer work on African Mythology collected and analysed about two thousand five hundred myths. He presented them as a guide to interpret African Traditional Religion and Culture.

He saw myths

as the objective and permanent philosophy of life of any given people.

(Baumann quoted by Smith, 1950, p. 6)

This book continued to serve as a very rich reference source for a long time. It was the first to be compiled by a diligent scholar who made serious efforts to reach the original owners of the myths. In spite of some flaws in trying to use western conceptual scheme to interpret his data, Baumann made a very brilliant effort in his presentation of facts. He travelled wide and made efforts to collect data that could be described as representative of myths from all over Africa. It was the first to be done on a continental level –though a few overgeneralizations and sweeping statements could be seen in some parts of the book. Many renowned writers have extensively used this work.

From the foregoing general discussions on myths, we may deduce a few points that relate to Igbo myths as our specific focus of study. In the first place, the philosophical and moral values embedded in the tales we intend to analyse are overwhelming. A systematic collection of such saga in Igbo society is not only long overdue but is also a valuable contribution to the ongoing quest for search for meaning and for a clearer ethical guide in the post-modern era of quagmire of moral confusion, loss of values, lack of respect for integrity, abuse of wealth and excessive pursuit of wealth without recourse to conscience and respect for cherished ancestral and traditional landmarks of values. Myths according to some of the scholars referred to above are generally understood as an important aspect of religion that gave values to societal ethos. This is because they primarily deal in the most practical terms with certain invisible and otherwise inexplicable facts of life. They serve as means of explanations of fact of life or certain practices and beliefs.

Secondly, to the Igbo, myths are different from other tales probably because they are believed to be substantially true (as Vansina has stated of myths generally) by those among whom they are repeated. They differ from two other kinds of tales that are not accorded equal respect. In other words, the Igbo distinguish folk-tales (Akuko *Ifo* or *Akuko Ilo*) from myths. Folk-tales are told for entertainment during moonlight plays, (Egwu *onwa)* although they may have some morals to teach. The Igbo also distinguish between myths from legends- (*Akuko gboo, Akuko Agba Ochie, Akuko mgbaka), which* are concerned with the history of the distant past.

We must at this juncture, make some clarifications on the terms used by Parrinder whom we have quoted earlier. He stated that legends refer to historical persons. Some of the Igbo myths recorded in text refer to specific names. On further enquiry in the sub-culture areas from where they were collected, we discovered that such names had no historical significance and basis as no elder was able to point to specific dates. So the names were more of symbolic figures and should be understood as such. In our interpretations, we did not belabour this fact. The truth of what they meant to the society is not diminished by this fact.

Thirdly, myths among the Igbo can be aptly called *Akuko maka Omenala*- implying stories about customs and traditions- aetiological stories. Not many scholars will agree on this but many elders would emphasise this as the real meaning of myths. They are basically concerned with traditions and tell sacred history (just as Benjamin Ray had stated). In spite of the attempts to clarify matters, we must, however, state that sometimes it is not easy to draw a definite line between myths and one form of the tales or the other especially as we moved from one subculture area to the other. They are all in oral form. Although some folk-tales may be called stories with songs, it is likely that they may be myths in making or survival of broken-down myths.

Similarly, myths and history are not easily distinguishable in a non-classical society like the Igbo we are studying. Those who tell them often believe them to have got historical foundation. We encountered this problem while listening to and analysing some of the myths of Creation from the Nri people of Northwest Igbo subculture area. It is probable that the distinctive sacred attribute of the *Nri Priest King* has made some scholars look at myths *in primitive societies as a pragmatic charter for primitive faith and moral wisdom* (Malinowski, 1954, p 107)

Just as C.G. Jung had stated, myths bear a stamp of antiquity. Since they have served as objective and permanent philosophy of life of any given people, myths have become the bedrock of cosmological explanations. In primary societies where the worldview is basically religious, myths have been used to back up the antiquity of any aspect of culture. Invariably, religious activities, taboos, customs, rituals and traditions are validated with myths.

Some myths can be said to be ideological- that is to say, they were invented to explain certain phenomena, beliefs and customs. They relate how one state of affairs became the other- how immortals became mortals, how the empty world became populated, how and why some events happen and etc. Their contribution toward enhancing the understanding of African Traditional Religion in general and Igbo religion in particular is immense.

THE IGBO- A SKETCHY ETHNOGRAPHY

The Igbo whose myths we intend to interpret in this work occupy the Southeastern part of Nigeria. They are one of the largest three ethnic groups in Nigeria and by and large one of the most widely spread and travelled single ethnic group in Africa. Their current estimate is 50 million based on the projection from the last census. Over ten million live in other parts of the world. They are known for their high achievement skill and their willingness to travel. They are so development-oriented that wherever they sojourn, they build it up as if it is their permanent home. Thus they scarcely discriminate against people or places. Their interest is just to see that places and people are made to move up the social ladder through self-effort and hard work.

They share common boundary with the Edo in the West, Ijaw and Kalabari in the South, the Idoma and Igala in the Northwest, the Tiv and Ogoja in the Northeast. At the Southeast border are the Ibibio (particularly the Annang subgroup) of the present Akwa Ibom State of Nigeria.

The present Abia, Anambra, Ebonyi, Enugu and Imo States have the largest concentration of Igbo population. They are the main areas we shall concentrate in this study. A sizeable population of the Igbo live in Rivers, Delta and part of Akwa Ibom States of Nigeria as their original home from prehistoric times. In the Rivers State they occupy the mainland areas of Ikwerre, Oyigbo, Etche, Ahoada, Omoku and Andoni. In Delta State, they occupy the Asaba, Kwale (Ukwani), Agbor, Iselle Ukwu, Obiaruku, Ibuza, (Igbo-uzo), and Utagba-Ogbe, Utagba-Uno, areas. In these areas they speak their own form of Igbo dialects. They however, speak and understand the Central Igbo Dialect, which is the official version of the language, which the electronic and print media use.

The political climate of the 1960s and post Nigeria/Biafran War era have made most of these Igbo areas claim that they are no Igbo at all. Some have been brainwashed to deny their Igbo roots as a way to get a fair share of the *National Cake* in other parts of Nigeria. Most of these areas have been intentionally carved into other non-Igbo territories to fragment the Igbo geographical area from being too large to cause trouble in Nigeria. Besides, they were carved out of the core Igbo area and ceded to some other ethnic groups and states to build up those areas. Some of them feel they have more opportunities to enjoy the benefits from the Federal system in those areas as they integrate with their non-Igbo speaking neighbours who still treat them as Igbo in disguise. Unfortunately, many of the original marks and attributes that make them Igbo are either carefully being removed or intentionally changed and mutilated to make them feel that they are no longer *Ndi-Igbo* (Igbo people). For instance, the names of some of the villages are spelt differently and some are completely given new names. Oyigbo now in Rivers State, which used to be Obigbo (Uriebe), got a new name when it was carved out of the then Igbo political territory. Part of the present Ikot-Abasi in Akwa Ibom State was pre- Nigeria /Biafra War part of Azumini in Ndoki area of Igboland. Some Opobo villages, which know they are descendants of Igbo stock, have been made to reject their Igbo connections and background.

The Igbo have established large communities in many parts of West Africa where they have been contributing immensely to socio-economic and religious developments of the areas where they sojourn. They have not been making much impact politically in those areas, as they are naturally not very keen politicians but business people, skilful artisans, independent entrepreneurs and urban and rural community development zealots.

The economy of the Igbo is still rural and subsistence agriculture the main occupation of majority. There are a few who through contact with Western education and civilization, have come to imbibe western life style. Industrialization and urbanization have been making steady impacts on the rural communities, which through community efforts built good roads, electricity, portable water supply, hospitals, schools and commercial markets. The importance of Self-Help Projects and Community Development Efforts ranks high in Igbo scale of preference and assessment of values. Consequently they do not wait for the regional or central government establishments to build any infrastructure for the local communities. They embark on such self-help efforts by levying themselves and building up their communities. That is why the Igbo are the first ethnic group in Africa that can be associated with building an Airport, university, industrial village, rural electricity projects, etc. which are still functioning.

Christianity is the *Official Religion* of many but the Traditional Religion still commands some respect in times of need and difficulty. In other words, Christianity is the dominant religion of the people and many world top Christian religious leaders have come from this part of the world. Islam has not got root in the land and traditional religion is dying out. Yet there are people who secretly patronize practitioners of the Igbo ancestral faith in times of extreme need. Many highly educated and well-placed Igbo in top executive positions may revert to seek the help of a traditional religious diviner, healer, or fortune teller in times of sickness that defies orthodox medical treatment, crises in place of work, progress in business or victory in election or success in examinations. Childlessness is another area of difficulty where many seek the help of the traditional religious functionaries.

The meaning of the word ***Igbo*** and the origin of the people have been an age long speculative problem involving anthropologists, ethnographers, culture-historians and linguists. It is now an overlaboured issue as well as an unsettled one. It is, therefore, beyond the scope of this study. The present writer had done a lot of work on that in one of his previous books (See Udobata Onunwa 1984 p. 10 – 30). The elders still claim that the Igbo are the original inhabitants of their present place of abode. Some late theories of Hebrew link are yet to be confirmed with authentic ethnographic data. Many believe that the Igbo are among the oldest stock of humanity and have not migrated from any other part of the universe to their present place.

The word Igbo stands for the people and their language. Another version - Ibo- (or Heebo) may be found in old books and records kept by colonial administrators and missionaries. Indigenous Igbo scholars and organisations have come to emphasise the use of the original and correct version of the word - **Igbo**. This is the version the elders and owners of the language and the people themselves use. The effort to bring the original and correct version into classical use was pioneered and sponsored by the Society for the Promotion of Igbo Language and Culture (S.P.I.L.C). Of late, it has gained the support of Igbo Unions in many parts of the world, particularly, the Apex Igbo Organisation – the **Ohaneze Ndi Igbo,** Igbo World Congress, Igbo Forum, Igbo Youth Movement, traditional rulers, church dignitaries, politicians, among others, have taken up the gauntlet. It is the version- Igbo- that we shall use in this book unless where we are quoting an old record kept by the missionaries or other Western scholars.

METHOD OF DATA COLLECTION, ANALYSIS AND PROBLEMS

The materials for this book were collected through primary fieldwork of five years. We depended heavily on oral primary source. We however, referred to a number of secondary sources by looking at the scanty work on myths by early European scholars. We also looked at the radio and television programmes of some of the Broadcasting Houses in Igbo territory and examined a few documents in the various departments of religion, history and linguistics of a few colleges where Igbo Language and Culture are offered as academic discipline.

During the field trips, we visited the five Igbo Subculture areas and other Igbo communities in the Rivers, Delta and Akwa Ibom States. Some students from the departments of history, religion, anthropology, political science, sociology, languages and linguistics from the various subculture areas acted as field assistants and interpreters. Some of them conducted the interviews themselves when we visited the religious functionaries, elders, community leaders and **Ndi-Eze** (traditional royal fathers).

We collected over a thousand tales and stories of wisdom. We sorted them out and created a careful taxonomy of the stories. We dropped a good number of them, which we felt did not fall within the group of myths in our taxonomy. Others were classified under several areas of life including agriculture, creation, marriage, family life, occupation, market, death, life, rites of passage, sickness, music, festivals, warfare, ecology, human destiny, life after death, sexual orientation, etc The system of classification or taxonomy, reduced the number of myths within some groups to a bare minimum and hence has created the unequal number of myths in each chapter of the book. It does not mean that there are no myths in some areas of life but we have tried not to duplicate a particular myth in another area of human life. One area of life where we were unable to discover a myth that explains it, is the End of the World or in biblical terms the Eschatology. The Igbo have myths about Creation and Origin of human life and nature but none for the end of the world. We considered it superfluous to repeat any particular version of myth that appears in several forms in many other places. For instance a myth from a particular subculture area or village may be used to explain why dogs live in human houses and lions in the forest. In another village, the same myth may be used to explain why dogs eat faeces and yet have white set of teeth and goats, which eat leaves, have dark and brown teeth. We have tried to write down the popular and widely circulated myths. Where another community has a different myth for a particular incident we document it but if it is a different version of the same myth, we only refer to the differences in the commentary without necessarily repeating the other version in full. This is to check unnecessary repetition. We have indicated the community from where we collected each version of myth recorded in the book. It does not mean that similar myths do not exist in other places.

The collection and analysis of the myths recorded here is not a simple job. As earlier stated, the Igbo like many other Africans speak in an oblique allusion which can confuse a stranger, and even a fellow Igbo person from another subculture area. The elders who narrated the tales spoke in their own local dialects and we have tried to retain such dialects in order to maintain the integrity of this work and also to guard against intellectual dishonesty. We were strict with some overzealous and literate interpreters from some villages who occasionally tried to distort the original version told by an illiterate elder by either trying to add some embellishments or polish the local dialect. We were careful and attentive when listening to the original version of the tales. When any tale sounded incoherent or incomprehensible, we asked the narrator to be either slow or to repeat the section that we did not fully understand. Our tape recorders were properly adjusted. We did not edit them but put down what the original owners of the myths said.

The other problem we encountered was how to distinguish between myth and history, or between myth and legend. We have stated above that the Igbo know the difference between these genres of oral saga. It must be emphasised here that not many could easily decipher the difference between one genre and the other.

Many elders muddled up the tales. An unwary investigator or enquirer might get confused or deceived. That is one of the advantages of working in an area with indigenous field assistants who understand the local culture and language thoroughly. We used the local language for the research and did not need middlemen to translate the tales for us. We listened directly from the narrators.

The present writer has two principal aims for carrying out this work. The first is to recapture as accurately as possible and without bias, the sacred tales of the Igbo still circulating in oral form in the various subculture areas. This is urgent now more than ever before because the tales get more and more adulterated and distorted in the process of transmission from one generation to the other. Some urgent work needs to be done along this line as a part of the ongoing projects to save the Igbo heritage and cultural wisdom from being either completely distorted, or lost to a large number of our children born and bred in urban centres and in Diaspora. It is both timely and expedient for one deeply involved in research and teaching of Igbo Institutions and Culture to make this contribution to the growing discipline of Igbo Studies. It is a very helpful contribution to document such repository of Igbo Wisdom and Civilization for generations yet unborn.

Secondly, the book will add to the existing number of source materials for our students in the universities, polytechnics, colleges of education and theological colleges who are studying African Traditional Religion, Sociology, Anthropology, Ethnography, Cultural and Media

Arts, Literature and Drama as academic discipline. For that reason, the text is simply written so that even young students would easily understand it. It is not surprising, especially to the present writer, to discover a good number of brilliant undergraduate students who know much about Greek, Hebrew and Western mythology through the Internet and literature, yet ignorant of their own indigenous African myths primarily due to lack of source materials. This book tries to make some of the myths and tales available to them in an orderly and well-written and systematically arranged form. A general reader as well as mature scholars will also benefit from it as a source of information on this genre of literature and philosophy, which has shaped a people's life and thought. In addition to this, policy makers, administrators, public opinion analysts, community development officers, play writers and theatre artists might learn much from the traditional cultural landscape of a people with whom they will come in contact at different times and for different purposes.

The present writer has a number of advantages in undertaking this work. He does not only understand Igbo Language and Culture but is an Igbo himself. He has, therefore, the privilege of listening directly to the elders as they narrated the tales just as has already been mentioned above. The cosmological views transmitted through the tales are not strange to him. Besides, his experience as a teacher and researcher in African Studies offered him opportunity to carry fieldwork with undergraduate and post-graduate students in universities in Nigeria, Tanzania, United Kingdom, India, Singapore and the United States on a wide range of topics. This position offered him opportunity to write in plain and simple language that is void of technical jargons that would either confuse young readers or non-professionals in the discipline.

Culture-Area and Phenomenological Approach is considered a viable methodological stance in doing this study. The Culture-Area emphasis takes care of the over-generalisation, which has been the bane of some of the previous works on Africa. The Phenomenological stance, on the other hand, takes care of the interpretation and hermeneutics. Although the narrators did not give any interpretation or commentary on their tales, we have attempted to do so. That is why we have chosen Phenomenological approach as our interpretation tool to avoid imposing our own views on the materials but have allowed the materials to explain and speak for themselves.

The narratives were originally presented in vernacular, in the very dialect of the people who told them. We have as much as possible retained the local dialects whenever we put down the vernacular version of the tales. This is just to enable the reader to appreciate its originality and aesthetics. We have, however, tried to render meaningful and contextual translation of the myths without impairing their original meaning and logic.

As a pioneer effort, this work does not in any way claim to be exhaustive. It is rather, a little scratch at the rich mine of Igbo repository of knowledge and wisdom. It would hopefully, serve as a humble contribution to the ongoing efforts by many indigenous Igbo scholars to update Igbo Studies, -especially Igbo History, Religion, Philosophy, Economics, Technology, Agriculture, Arts, Medicine, Pharmacology, Architecture and Science. This revised and enlarged edition depended much on the corrections, criticisms and suggestions from readers and friends who used the original and first edition.

Finally, we have to remark that it is important that African countries and in fact other Third World Nations in this 21st Century who are seriously planning to entrench peaceful, clean and honest government in their lands, must go back to their ancient roots and retrieve some valuable aspects of their noble past as revealed in their sacred tales and philosophy. They should also examine themselves and their cultures critically to know areas that need pruning or to be expunged; especially areas that have hindered growth, sustainable democracy and development, economic freedom and social justice. The myths of the Igbo of the West African sub-region herein collected, analysed and interpreted depict an ancient civilization of thousands of years whose technology, medicine, agriculture, engineering, traditional government, and ethical norms that were highly developed but abandoned some time along the line. The presence of some external change agents gradually eroded the cherished values that built a community. Some eternal values can be retrieved from the culture for building a cherished and peaceful society.

A close study of the vestigial remains of ancient Igbo Civilization, validated in their myths herein examined, confirms the extent of the development of their ***Lost Paradise***. The gauntlet is now thrown to current policy makers in post-modern era and nationalists in Africa and Igboland in particular to recapture their lost sense of direction and glory. The legacies of the ancestral founding fathers that led to the invention of a lot of wonderful works of art and science must be recaptured if any meaningful technological and industrial take-off will be made in this post-modern time.

ACKNOWLEDGEMENT

This work, which grew out of a large chunk of data collected from an extensive fieldwork of five years, involved a lot of people, patience and effort. It took both time and money. The long period of data collection offered us immense opportunities to visit many parts of the territory to experience at first hand, a wide range of Igbo Traditional socio- political, economic and religious changes going on in the various subculture areas. A good number of experienced and respectable Igbo traditional rulers, religious specialists and functionaries, chiefs, elders and leaders offered help and guidance at various points in time and places. Many people contributed to see this book see the light of day. For convenience, we intend to classify them into two main groups.

The first is made up of the veritable elders, religious experts, Ndi-Eze, (Traditional Rulers), in the various Igbo sub-culture areas who allowed us to visit them or to attend the festivals of their communities. They were patient enough to narrate the myths when we called on them. It was a privilege to meet some of the highly revered sacred priests at their shrines. It was also a great privilege to be granted the permission to meet some of the highly respected and busy monarchs in their palaces. On some occasions, we disturbed a number of them and took them away from their previously arranged programme especially when we called without previous appointment. They offered us the traditional Igbo hospitality and blessed the work we told them we were doing. These men and women earned our respect and they did more than can be fully acknowledged here. They did not ask for the usual financial gratification for offering useful information to field research workers. Their only demand was to make sure that we do not distort the stories and also to make sure that the work is published.

The other group is made up of my past students at the University of Nigeria, Nsukka and the University of Calabar, academic colleagues and friends. Some of the students who took part in the fieldwork finished their postgraduate work a few years ago and in fact are teaching in some other universities now. The students continued to challenge me to put down in a systematic order all that we have been discussing in the classroom, seminar room and tutorials on myths in primeval societies. Besides that initial challenge, some of them brought their colleagues from the Departments of English, Literary Studies, Education, Anthropology, Sociology, History, and Theatre Arts, who joined us in our field trips. Often many of them missed their meals and lectures in the other courses when we stayed too long in a particular village. I really owe them a debt of gratitude that can hardly be repaid. There is no greater stimulus or any greater reward for a committed teacher than the response of awakened minds. Some of the students were so enthusiastic that they carefully conducted the field research in their own local communities during the holiday and brought us back the tapes and photos. We, however, revisited the places to validate and confirm the data. In many of the trips, they acted as interpreters of local dialects that did not represent the Central Igbo Dialect and accent

A few people who did extra work on this include J.C Akubueze, E. C. Nwangwu, E. Odo, Humphrey Eze, Innocent Onyeishi, Eze Nwaonu Eze, Fidelia Munonye, Cate Okeosisi, Evelyn Anyadike, Adline Okere, Augustine Osakwe, Augustine Ekeopara, Greg Nwakoby, Andrew Okenwa, Emmanuel C. Ilogu, Goodwill Ukwuoma and Rebecca Egwu. I want to thank Pacific Publishers Obosi Nigeria for the excellent work they did on my two previous books. Thy published my works without asking for printing subsidy.

A few colleagues who read the manuscripts and suggested helpful changes include O.M. Anizoba, Herbert Anyanwu, G.E. Okeke, S.C.Chuta, E.M. Uka, Igwe Aja-Nwachukwu, Fr Innocent Asuzu and Professor N.S.S. Iweh. Mrs Eno Nta of the Department of English and Literary Studies, University of Calabar, helped me as my stylistic consultant. She polished the language of the text and cleaned off all the wrong expressions and spellings. Professor Ogbu U. Kalu was helpful with the suggestion on the Methodology to use for the analysis while my former dean Professor Kalu Uka helped with research grants that funded part of the fieldwork. I also thank Professor Edmund Ilogu who taught me methods of social research in religion and continued to encourage me during my undergraduate days in the university.

Finally, I want to thank my brother Iyk Onunwa of the Department of History who organised all the field trips and the papers. My wife Dorothy has done more than can be acknowledged here. In spite of her own heavy professional load in the hospital, she was generous enough to offer hospitality each time I brought home my field assistants. She provided the convenient home environment to which we retired at the end of our field trips. Besides, she provided the financial support that took me to London twice to look for materials at the libraries of the School of Oriental and African Studies (S.O.A.S) and the Museum. There, I was privileged to meet with my old mentor, the retired Professor E. G. Parrinder who looked at the drafts and restructured the chapters.

Udobata R. Onunwa
University of Nigeria, Nsukka

Post Script.
It is indeed my joy to record my indebtedness to Thesen Verlag of Germany for an unprecedented interest shown in publishing this work. As soon as I contacted them about it, they sent me a telegram to forward the manuscripts for evaluation. Thereafter, they approved it and embarked on production. Pacific Publishers had earlier done excellent work on my three other books.

Preface to the Revised Edition

African Studies had grown in many ways since the first edition of this work was published in Germany. Many authors are unearthing some hitherto hidden materials that need to be included in any strong academic research work. We have made several additions, which invariably enlarged the original volume. We have equally seen the extension of scale in the areas where the original fieldwork was conducted. We have taken note of the several structural changes in Igbo World since then. The cultural landscape has changed tremendously and this work has taken note of that. The current geo-political changes going on in the Igbo world have helped us to reinterpret some of the myths in the context of current events and experiences. Many associations have come up among the Igbo in Africa and those in Diaspora, each looking for identity, support, and direction. It is their cultural heritage that many of them cling to for support in times of confusion and in their quest for corporate and individual identity.

The new national consciousness of many pressure groups of Igbo extraction in different parts of the world has enlarged Igbo philosophy and political ideology in contemporary times. Their vision of their world is invariably enlarging. The work of Igbo World Congress in the United States of America has given a new impetus to this Igbo new consciousness and people want to be identified as ***Ndi- Igbo*** i.e. Igbo people wherever they meet and talk. The try to emphasize Igbo values and articulate Igbo philosophy. We have included this new concept of life in our comments on some of the meanings and interpretations of the myths in contemporary times. The Igbo in Midlands UK have also embarked on a very organised high profile quest for Igbo identity and place in comity of nations. The City Council has recognised the Iwa-ji Festival as an important contribution to the growth of Birmingham as a multi-ethnic, multi-religious and multi-cultural centre of Europe. The holiday language course, cultural studies, and dances, which the Igbo organise in Birmingham, is now a well established annual programme. Many people have enjoyed it- young, old, little school pupils, diplomats, foreign wives married to proud Igbo nation, missionaries, businessmen, etc now want to know more of the Igbo in the world.

Udobata Onunwa
Birmingham UK
2005

CHAPTER ONE
MYTHS OF CREATION

1.1. Creation Myth from Nri
(Northwest Igbo Subculture Area)

The Nri traditions of origin circulate in the north and northwest Igbo subculture areas. People in these areas believe that Nri is the Cradle of Human Civilization in general and Igbo culture in particular. The tradition asserts that when Eri came down to earth from the sky, he sat on an anthill as the land was a morass or waterlogged *Ala di deke-deke.* He was sent down from the sky with his wife Namuaku. (A version said he had a second wife whose name was Oboli who bore Onoja who left the Anambra Basin to found the Igala- land. (We shall come to this later).

Following Eri's complaint, Chukwu- the Supreme God- sent down an Awka blacksmith who used his fiery bellows to dry up the land. When Eri was alive, Chukwu fed him and his dependants. They were fed on *Azu Igwe* (a type of fish from the back of the sky). The food supply from Chukwu was terminated on the death of Eri. Then his eldest son, Nri, petitioned Chukwu about the precarious situation of hunger and acute food shortage. He was instructed to kill and bury in separate graves, his first son and daughter. After trying in vain to evade the command, Nri complied and carried out the order. Consequently, after three Igbo weeks (Izu Ato) i.e. twelve days, yam sprouted from the grave of the son and cocoyam from that of the daughter. When Nri and his people ate the new food supply, they slept for the first time.

Later still, Nri killed one of his male slaves and a female slave too. He buried them in separate graves as he did previously. Accordingly, after *Izu- Ato*, (three Igbo native weeks, which is twelve days), an oil palm tree (nkwu) grew up from the grave of the male slave and breadfruit tree – (ukwa) sprang up from that of the female slave.

Nri and his people prospered because of the new food supply. He was ordered again by Chukwu to distribute the new food items to all mankind. Nri objected, arguing that he had paid dearly for them by sacrificing his son and daughter in the first instance and two slaves in addition. Eventually again, he yielded and an accord was reached. For accepting to distribute the food items to other peoples in the known universe, Chukwu agreed to reward Nri with several rights and privileges over the surrounding neighbourhood. He was thenceforth given the right to cleanse every town and community of any abomination committed in it, and to tie the *Ngwulu* (a sacred ankle cord) on men who took Ozo titles, and to crown kings at Aguleri. The Ozo title is the highest honorific title, which is conferred on men of honour and integrity and transparent honesty in different parts of Igboland. In addition to all these benefits, Nri was also given Ogwu – Ji (medicine for yam production) in order to ensure a rich harvest of yams every year in all the neighbouring towns including the towns that submitted themselves to the Eze-Nri (the King of Nri). Thenceforth, the Umunri, i.e. the descendants of Nri who constituted themselves into a big town received tributes from the neighbouring communities. They travelled throughout the world (Igbo known world) unmolested and became purveyors of cults, civilisation and crafts. That immunity made the Umunri ubiquitous medicine men, healers, priests, advisers, harbingers and purveyors of skills and development Then the Igbo knack for business and long adventure began. The ***Umunri- ndi oje n'mmuo***- believed to be travellers from and to the Spirit World or visitors from there- sojourned all over the world as herbalists and doctors without being molested.

COMMENTS:

The myth tells of significant beginnings.

(a)   the creation of the solid earth

(b)   the origin of basic food items

(c)   the origin of sleep and death- though some other myths in the text point to the origin of death in a different context.

(d)   The myth also points to the establishment of the relationship between Nri, Awka and the other surrounding peoples.

Secondly, it obviously articulates aspects of Igbo world-view and values, e.g. the Igbo ideas of the effort at bargaining expressed in the fact that Nri had to complain to Chukwu – the Supreme God, before he (Chukwu) could help his people and in Nri's bargaining with Chukwu over the terms for the distribution of the food items to other peoples in the world. This may also point to Igbo person's boldness to question any leader particularly when a matter concerning his welfare is concerned. No Igbo would like to be taken for granted when any issue concerning his personal welfare and interest is being discussed. His boldness to ask questions is depicted in this myth. He respects any one in authority but does not fear him. He knows the difference between fear and honest respect of institutions and authorities. The significance of yam and palm tree as male crops is hereby validated. Similarly, cocoyam (ede) and breadfruit tree (ukwa) are known as female crops.

Thirdly the myth expresses the relationship between a man and Chukwu. God is the Divine Power behind the world, man and society and the provider of all human needs. But even Chukwu can be bargained with and often manipulated showing that the Igbo worldview of humanity's relationship with the Sacred and Divine Beings is not fatalistic. The Igbo attitude to political and religious authorities is mixed with respect and boldness. He questions boldly if a matter is either not clear or proves unacceptable to him.

The Nri Myth, which evolves from what, the modern Igbo Studies describe as Anambra Civilization was sustained in yam cultivation and developed a complex body of theological beliefs based on both monotheistic and polytheistic dogmas. These include Chukwu as the Creator of all things- Okike; Chukwu as the Source of Fertility-*agbala*; Chukwu as the Source of light and knowledge- *Anyanwu*. Chukwu is the source of procreation- *Chi;* etc. The custodian of this system of religious dogma and doctrine is the Eze-Nri, who on his coronation died, *buried, and rose again* symbolically and ritually. This process transformed him into *Nmuo- Spirit-* or god. It was he alone in the distant past who had the power to abrogate or enact rule of avoidance- taboo, forbidden traditions, *Nso-Ana (Nso- Ala)*, and rules of abominations- *Alu (Aru)*. He had the single power to control the fertility of yam through performance of rituals that control yam pests and insects like locusts, or ecological problems like drought. These were embodied into the corpus called Ogwu-Ji- (Medicine for yam production and preservation). These powers of Nri were enacted and reinforced by the annual festival of **Igu-Aro**. Different versions of this sacred dogma are found in different parts of Igbo land but none is as developed in a clearly thought-out and systematic theological order as it is found in Nri Myth.

Surprisingly, the myth is silent over the role of Namuaku or Oboli – the wives of Eri in the development of the events and the activities of humans on earth. It is not out to explain marriage as a monogamous or polygamous practice. None of the two women is mentioned as either the source of good or evil in the world, nor as a helpmate or stumbling block to Eri's relationship with Chukwu. Some other Igbo myths speak of man's loss of bliss and privilege on account of the errors of a woman but never attribute any of the errors to either Namuaku or Oboli.

Fourthly, we have to note that some historical events are given a cosmic significance, for instance the origin of agriculture and of iron production and smelting.

Finally, the myth is also a social charter, legitimising the ritual and socio-political authority of Nri people over surrounding Igbo known world. Those who ascribe the origin of any highly developed institutions in Igboland to sources outside Igboland cannot stand the challenge of Nri Myths. It is implied that one of the wives of Nri called Oboli was the mother of Onuju who later became the ancestral founding father of the Igala. In other words, the Igala took their origin from the Igbo. The same is believed of other human beings on earth according to some elders in Igboland. The myth underscores the age of the Igbo race as a people in the universe. They claim to be the oldest human race- the Original Humanity. An acronym states that the meaning of the name **IGBO** is *I – Go- Before- Others* or **IBO**- *(I Before Others*) indicating the primacy of the Igbo race in the universe, *I existed before others, I was created before others*. Those who hate the Igbo ways of life and character as well as critics of Igbo progress and knack for business and their enterprising spirit interpret it to mean that the Igbo are *selfish or greedy*, characteristics abhorrent to Igbo humane living and altruistic nature. The Igbo are to say the least not greedy or selfish but republican and independent in their outlook. The Nri myth is Igbo interpretation of both their history and that of mankind in general. The Igbo usually describe all Blacks as Igbo *People* The Igbo think that every black person is an Igbo and that makes them show love and kindness to people. That is one of the reasons behind their friendly attitude to people and willingness to live among any people believing that they are their kiths and kin. That is the origin of the Igbo proverb, which states that *'Nwanne di n'mba'* implying that one's relatives are found everywhere or somewhere else. So they encourage people to try to show kindness to those around them whether strangers or close relatives. You have some of your relatives in other places too. The Igbo have for long assumed that since the Black is the first and most dominant colour, 'stronger *and older colour'* all other human races of various skin pigmentation are *younger* than the Igbo- thus they emphasize the primacy of the Igbo world and people as the original humanity.

1.2.   Edo Deity and the Creation of the Solid Earth
(Version from Nnewi in the Northwest Igbo Subculture Area)

Edo is a female deity who lived in the sky with Chukwu in the distant past. She found special favour with Chukwu because she was very beautiful and industrious. Consequently, Chukwu gave her his staff of office, a piece of sceptre made of while chalk, (*nzu*), and small clay pot of water and asked her to survey the firmament. Unfortunately during the spatial trip, Edo lost her way and was carried beyond the firmament. She found herself stranded in an unknown open space. Instead of being idle and bemoaning her predicament, as an industrious personality, she began to grind the white chalk (nzu) and spread the powder on the marshy surface that covered everywhere. The chalk dried and covered the marshy areas and thus formed the solid earth. She broke the remaining part of the chalk into four parts and put them in the pot. When Chukwu found her tired and completely knackered and sitting alone on the land, he took pity on her. He decided to send her some companions to help her to run errands and do some work for her. Thus Chukwu brought out the four pieces of the chalk from the pot and placed them at various locations and gave them the following names:

i.   Otolo
ii.   Uruagu
iii. Umudim
iv.   Ichi

Chukwu breathed into them and they turned into human beings and they became the founding fathers of the four major villages in Nnewi today. They became the four sons of Edo Deity and thus called their land Ana- Edo meaning the Land of Edo Deity. When they grew up to marry, they went to Arochukwu in the South-east Igbo subculture area and picked up four beautiful girls who happened to come from the same parents. Through them, the four Edo sons raised children that became the indigenous inhabitants of Nnewi.

COMMENTS

The myth acknowledges that humans were created after the creation of the solid earth. He came up to see the earth in existence. The industrious nature of Edo Deity may be the reason for her being loved by Chukwu who is known to bless those who work very hard, just like he does. The Igbo believe that those in authority always like a hard-working person. Hard work is the key to success. Laziness is the root of poverty and misery.

Nnewi is known to be a town of hardworking and enterprising people who have been successful in many areas of human endeavour. This is probably attributable to their Town Patron Deity – Edo- who is revered in the community. The myth tries to establish a link between the Aro and Nnewi- two communities Igboland known for their shrewdness in business entrepreneurship. There is no solid ethnographic data for one to validate the claim that the Aros and Nnewi had such links in prehistoric times.

The Aro willingness to spread far into any part of the Igbo world is reflected in the willingness of the four young girls to agree to marry far away from their home. The practice of exogamic marriage is common in many Igbo communities.

1.3   The Age of the Solid Earth.
(Version from Enugwu-Ukwu, Northwest Igbo Subculture Area)

Chukwu wanted to create the solid earth by using some animals as his agents. He sent them to do the work instead of doing it directly by himself. Man had not been created by then and therefore did not know the exact time Chukwu did it. The solid earth surface had been in existence before Chukwu created the first humans. Since there was no calendar, humans did not know the oldest of the creatures and the age of the solid earth itself.

The Council of Elders and Ozo Title Holders met to discuss the age of the earth and how it came into existence. The oldest man could not account for it. He expressed ignorance of the method and time when Chukwu did the work. The council decided to consult an Oracle- *Dibia Afa* to enquire from him when and how Chukwu created the earth. None of the Diviners could tell the exact date. One day, of the oldest men in the village overheard two animals quarrelling over who was older than the other The Chameleon (*Ogwumagana*) and the Kingfisher *(Okpoko)* had a dispute over which of them was older than the other.

In traditional African societies, seniority in age gave one an advantage over others in any assembly. Age is usually associated with wisdom and therefore the oldest person in a community is usually regarded as the wisest. The Chameleon stated in the council of the animals that he was older than the Kingfisher. He informed the assembly that this could be ascertained from the way he walks. He was born when the earth was a morass, too soft for any living creature to walk on briskly because *Ala di deke- deke-* meaning that the land surface was soft and marshy. He had to tip toe his walk in order to avoid sinking. He was very cautious and slow. It is the reason for his characteristic slow movement. When the earth became hardened, he was not sure it was strong enough for him to walk fast on it. He therefore did not change his steps but continued to walk slowly till today.

The Kingfisher, on the other hand, told the assembly that when he was born, everywhere was covered with water. His mother died suddenly and he was distressed. The funeral was fixed and his friends came to sympathise with him. Unfortunately, there was no solid ground for them to dig a grave to bury the mother's body. He moved around over a long time looking for an empty place that was dry and hard enough to use as a burial ground. While he was searching for a dry land, his father died also. He was compelled to carry the corpse also around but this second time on his beak. He was constrained to carry the two corpses around for a very long time- one on the head and the other on the beak – i.e. near its neck. Since then the Kingfisher is seen carrying two heavy loads, one on the head and the other on the neck. This has been the reason for the Kingfisher's big head and big neck. Neither the Chameleon nor the Kingfisher appealed to Chukwu to provide them a dry ground to carry out their business. The dispute ended there and none was able to convince the assembly of his seniority over the other. Man, could therefore, not ascertain which of the two was older nor how and when the earth surface was created.

COMMENTS

There is clear evidence that the original nature of the universe is hereby underlined. The difficulty in locating death is obvious in this myth since there is no other information on the origin of death but it is taken as a known phenomenon in this case. The struggle for pre-eminence of one creature over the other is inherent in any ecosystem. It is natural to fight for survival. The inability of one creature to establish its seniority over the other is an indication of the difficulty of placing created beings in their chronological order of creation as that is beside human comprehension.

Besides, it is characteristic of the harsh ecological environment in which people found themselves. It also points to the argument in recent times that the term *Okike-* creation-was not originally attributed to the Supreme Being in Igbo cosmology. That life began in water can be understood from many other myths, which indirectly refer to the marshy nature of the primeval world. The myth underscores Igbo sense of communal deliberations to take action on any matter that arises in the community.

1.4   Creation of Rain
(Version from Awka, Northwest Igbo Subculture Area)

When Chukwu created man after he had dried the marshy earth surface, he forgot to give rain to man immediately. The scarcity of rain continued for a long time and all the trees and plants started to die off. Consequently, no one cultivated the rich land and many people started to die of hunger and thirst as severe famine (ugani) ravished the whole land. As the situation worsened, the elders met and decided to send a delegation to Chukwu to ask him to send rain on earth. One of the birds, the hawk, (egbe) was sent by man to carry the message to Chukwu in the heavens.

The hawk is a fast flying bird. He got to the heavens in time and met Chukwu in his sitting room. He reported the human conditions on earth to the Supreme Being who sympathized with humans on hearing the sad news of their suffering. He decided on the spot to send rains to the earth. He wrapped water in a broad and fresh leaf of cocoyam plant and gave it to the hawk to deliver to man on earth. He advised the hawk to fly as fast as he could to take the parcel to suffering humanity on earth before they die of thirst and hunger.

The hawk has long and sharp claws. The claws tore open the leaves of the cocoyam in which the water was wrapped. Before long, the whole content of the parcel was emptied and poured down to earth before the hawk could reach home to man on earth. So from a very high altitude the water started pouring down on humans and their possessions on earth. It poured out so heavily that some roads got flooded; water percolated in some crevices and holes and became rivers and streams. Some holes were filled with water that fell from above and thus created seas and oceans. The hawk became frightened as he felt that the parcel given to him to deliver to man has been lost. He decided not to return to the earth again for fear of being lynched as a bad messenger.

He became afraid of rains and from that day decided to fly away to another part of the world where there is no rain falling. That was the reason behind the migration of hawks to dry regions during the rainy season in Igboland. They start to return to Igbo region during November and early December and stay till mid May and migrate again to other parts of the world during the rainy season. That is why we do not have hawks in Igboland during the rainy and wet season. The hawks began to dread the rains.

According to a version of this myth from Ideani in the same subculture area, rocks were very soft and the sky hung loose within the reach of man's hands. People standing on earth could cut out some pieces of the cloud and eat them.

An angry woman struck the white sky with a pestle and scattered the white clouds on one afternoon. As soon as the white clouds were hit by the woman's pestle, the sky broke open and poured out large quantity of water. Those around ran away for their dear lives when they saw the water pouring down from the sky. Since then, the clouds have continued to give signs of rains during the rainy season. Man standing outside his home has continued to run as fast as he could when it begins to rain. Those walking on the road ran fast to take shelter where they found houses to avoid being beaten by the rain when they saw it falling from the sky. No one walked leisurely on the road because the heavy drops of water were coming down from the sky.

COMMENTS.

The authority of man over other creatures is hereby confirmed. It is man who sent a messenger- the hawk to Chukwu. Besides, the ability of man to appeal or complain is here by emphasised again. The Igbo character of speaking out their minds is herein underlined. They sent an appeal to Chukwu to send rain.

The dry nature of the earth surface does not contradict the fact that the original earth surface was marshy and waterlogged. Many parts of the universe are still dry and have no natural running water like rivers and streams. They Igbo interpret migration of birds at certain seasons with this incident.

The version from Ideani seems to suggest that it was the fault of woman again that brought rain. This has nothing to do with the *Fall of Man* or the origin of sin. Some other myths that explain the loss of human bliss and close relationship with Chukwu exist. This myth is probably one of those that look for scapegoats for any error in human society and woman is often the chief culprit in a society that is male-dominated. Most of the elders who tell the myth were men.

1.5   Igwe, Ana and the Coming of Rain
(Myth from Alor, Idemili, Northwest Igbo Subculture Area.)

Chukwu has two **children** called Igwe and Ana (the sky and the earth). They were in constant quarrels and arguments common among siblings. The main issue was the dispute over who was the older among them. Their father or creator Chukwu did not tell them which was the older of the two. In traditional communities seniority in age places one in a very privileged position. So the two siblings- Igwe and Ana were struggling over who would inherit the larger share of their father's property.

Ana (the earth) boasted of what he can do and does in society. He controls every one living on the earth surface. He offers humans the opportunity to grow food and live a healthy life. It is on the earth surface that humans build their houses, play, and run around. At death, the earth provides humans a place to bury their corpses. So, all living creatures in the universe depend on the Earth for sustenance. The earth provides humanity all that he needs for existence in the world. He, therefore, claimed that judging by all that he provides to humans, he should be recognised as the older of the two. He went further to state that he provides the foundation on which the pillars that hold the sky and earth stand. So if the earth caved in, the sky would collapse. He should therefore, be recognised as Chuwku's first son- the **Okpala.**

Igwe (the sky) in his reply claimed that he controls all heavenly phenomena without which the earth collapses. Although human beings build their houses and plant their crops on earth, Igwe provides their life with sustenance that makes them life on earth possible. If the sky refuses to make any of his resources available to humans living on earth, life would be uncomfortable if not impossible. The sun will not shine, the moon will not come out and the rain will not fall. There will be total darkness and absolute drought. While the debate was going on, Igwe decided to temporarily withhold the rains from falling on the earth surface. Earth took it lightly and never bothered about it until humans suffering on earth petitioned *Chukwu and Igwe* to show mercy. After a few weeks, the sky sent out the sun with hot rays, which drew up all the moisture on the earth surface. Within a few weeks, the lakes, ponds, streams, rivers, and even big seas dried up. Trees lost their leaves and withered. The weather became unbearably too hot for living creatures on land and sea and many things died. Human beings begin to die of hunger, thirst and heat burns.

The elders consulted an oracle to enquire of the source of their misfortune. The diviner revealed to them the cause of the problem. Humans summoned an emergency meeting and they decided to plead with the Earth to kindly reconcile with his **brother** to save them from total annihilation. It was not easy for humans to get the message across to the Sky above. They finally prevailed on the Earth who unwillingly swallowed his pride and accepted the second position as the younger of the two. Humans decided to send one of the surviving birds, the Vulture, to take the message of Earth's surrender of position of seniority to Igwe above. When the vulture got up to the abode of the Sky, he delivered the message of surrender by the earth to Igwe- the Sky, who graciously accepted the offer and decided to rescind his strong decision to punish the earth and all who dwell on it.

As the Vulture set out for home to deliver the good news of Igwe's readiness to send rain to humans on earth, the Sky went into his inner chambers and released a large quantity of rain. It was so heavy that the vulture was caught up on his way and became badly drenched. Before he could reach home, the soaked vulture had lost most of his feathers. Since that day, the vulture began to hate the rains that made him lose his feathers. That is why the vulture does not have many feathers. The sky decided that he would not be sending rains as frequently as he did before the quarrel with the earth. He would be gracious enough to send it at certain months of the year and thereafter, close up again. That is why we have a season that is full of rain and another that is completely dry. Hence the birth of the two seasons – Rainy and Dry Seasons in Igbo land.

COMMENTS

The origin of the two major seasons in Igboland is hereby underlined by this myth- a quarrel between two siblings. The conflict and struggle in ecosystem which is a part of the **theory of evolution** is hereby underscored.

The gender struggle is also underlined-which seems to endorse dominant male supremacy over female The Igbo take Igwe- Sky as a male deity and the Earth- as a female deity. The expression ***Igwe na Ana raa***- i.e. ***Igwe and Ana copulate*** to produce living creatures. It is when Igwe fertilizes the Earth with the water of life- the rain, (invariably the sperm), that the earth becomes productive. The earth is below and the sky is on top just in the same position couples stay when they make babies. It is the one on top who is stronger and older! The earth is known in many Igbo myths as a Goddess- *the Mother Earth* represented as a benevolent mother. As a male-dominated society, the Igbo believe that male figure should predominate the female and hence the Igwe is regarded as male who suppressed the female earth. It is a man's world! This is not to justify the suppression of one gender over the other but states the roles of each personality, which should not be seen in terms of superiority or quality but in complementary terms. Unfortunately, many do not understand this idea of female/male complements. In a capitalistic philosophy, which supports winner-takes-all, seniority is expressed in an arrogant way. The myth underpins the fact that when two elephants fight, it is the grass that suffers. Many problems which humanity suffers in the universe are not necessarily caused by man's misuse of the natural order or abuse of nature. Many ecological disasters are cosmic and not all caused by human sin but occasionally as result of 'quarrels' between mystical bodies in the cosmos. Yet humans are expected to live pure and holy life so as not to provoke the anger of the deities and suffer for their misdemeanour. Human factors also contribute to sufferings and disruption in the ecosystem or natural world.

The quarrel can be seen from another perspective - the characteristic struggle for survival in natural ecology depicting indirect reference to the Igbo concept of evolutionary theory of the beginning of life. The struggle again may be a reference to the common feature of struggle to overtake a peer- common in capitalistic system where every one tries to overtake the other in a do or die competitive spirit.

The difference between Chukwu (the Supreme Being) and Igwe (Sky deity) is clearly stated here. The Sky or Igwe is not Igbo Supreme God who dwells above .He is not the sky god. He is CHI-UKWU who dwells *above but* not in the Sky! The idea of above is in terms of power, strength, purity, holiness, knowledge but not necessarily physical. The early European and Mission scholars who described the African God as *Deus Otiosus, or Deus Remotus or as Sky God* actually misunderstood the people's concept of God. This is particularly true of the Igbo concept of God. Igwe is not confused with *Chukwu* or *Chineke* or *Obasi Di N'elu – the Supreme God.* The Igwe deity, often times seen as *Igwe-Ka- Ala* meaning the *Sky is bigger than Earth*- the Oracular deity localized at Umunoha in the former Mbaitolu Local Government of Imo State. The operators of this oracle like those of the Ibin Ukpabi of Arochukwu used the terms Chukwu or Igwe to manipulate the credulous clients into believing that they were agents of the Supreme Deity- a fraudulent practice that disgraced Igbo integrity, honest religious belief and clean way of creating wealth. Both shrines were destroyed for their evil involvement in the notorious Slave Trade.

Although the Supreme Being, Chukwu, lives *above*, he is not a *sky god*. Man looks up to plead with Chukwu and he distinguishes between the sky above and the Chukwu who lives above the sky.

1.6. **Chukwu and the Birth of Seasons**
(Myth from the Isu-ama Subgroup of the South Igbo
subculture Area – the Igbo heartland)

The two eldest sons of Igwe decided that they would stop their mother from having more children after she had given birth to two more children- These were the *Udumiri* (Wet Season) and the *Okochi* (Dry Season).

Igwe had given birth to her first two children- Anyanwu (Sun) and Onwa (Moon) and both of them were happy till their mother gave birth to two other children – the Wet Season and the Dry Season. The two oldest siblings suggested to their mother that she should stop having more children. It was an abomination in Igbo world for a woman of viable childbearing age to stop when she is still potentially fertile. So it was not possible for them to convince their mother to stop at four. While the argument was still going on, Igwe became pregnant again and bore the fifth child who became naughty and rough and was not prepared to respect anyone including his mother. The name of this fifth child was called **Ifufe-** a wild strong hurricane wind that blows off people's houses and has no regards for anyone. Ifufe became too dangerous to people's thatched houses, blew down big trees like the Iroko and mahogany, etc. The sun and moon approached their mother again to stop having more babies. Igwe reasoned that five is an odd number and it is not proper for the Igbo to do with anything that does not go in pairs. So it would be necessary to have the sixth one so as to get the pairs in order. Igbo life goes in twos The next time, Igwe became pregnant and gave birth to a more vicious and dangerous child called Uguru- (Harmattan), a very dry and unfriendly weather which made human skins very dry and rough.

This was the most horrible weather the humans could stand. So the mother was compelled to stop at that. This last child brought a lot of problems too many people although it helped to make some trees get their flowers have cross-pollination by scattering them far and wide. The mother there and then stopped having more children. Igwe then had six children- Anyanwu (Sun), Onwa (Moon), Udumiri (Wet Season), Okochi (Dry Season), Ifufe (Strong Hurricane Wind) and Uguru (Harmattan). The two oldest children persuaded their mother not to allow any humans to worship the last four as gods. Hence people worship Anyanwu (sun god) and Onwa (moon god) but there is not cult of the Udumiri (Wet Season), Okochi (Dry Season), Ifufe (strong hurricane wind) and Uguru (harmattan).

COMMENTS

The motif of family planning is implied in this myth. The objection to adopt it initially is a reflection of the vehemence with which it is opposed even till today in post-modern Igbo society. No woman would like to stop having babies as far as she is viable. Many people in large families obviously complain of the problems the younger ones bring to the families and their neighbourhood. Hence the Sun and Moon do not cause as much problems to society as the rainy and dry seasons. This is worsened by the dangers hurricane wind and harmattan cause humans. Some people believe that the size of a family as well as age of parents are among the factors that can influence the level of discipline in it. The Igwe is presented here as a female deity, though in most Igbo myths, he is male. The myth is not out to project gender issue but to state the birth of seasons. It is believed that the Igbo do not like the debilitating effect of harmattan (uguru) on human skin, eyes, lips, etc yet they appreciate its contributions to agricultural success. Family planning among the Igbo is resisted even in their spiritual world and realm.

1.7 The Creation of Day and Night
(Myth from Ibagwa Nsukka, North Igbo Subculture Area, and version from Isiukwuato, Northeast Igbo Subculture Area)

Some time in the distant past, when there was neither day nor night, there was a man who built a very large compound where he lived with his many wives and children. He was quite rich and had a large estate where his numerous slaves and servants farmed for him. One of the wives was barren and the co-wives taunted her and ridiculed her just like as it is common in many traditional societies where high premium is paid on childbirth. Children are index of wealth and blessing. Incidentally, the childless woman was the most beloved wife of her husband and that generated a sort of jealousy among the other wives. Each time some of the co-wives would accuse her of being a witch or being wicked. It was her evil character that blocked her chances of having a child. She was depressed and most of the time crying. Her husband would console her and assure her of his constant love. She was found most of the time praying and pleading with *Obasi Di Nelu*- the *Ezechitoke*- the Supreme God just for one child and that would wipe out her tears and shame. It is believed in Igboland that a barren woman must have been a witch or a very wicked woman who is punished with barrenness by the Supreme Being for being wicked and devilish.

One day, the woman heard of a medicine man (Dibia) who could give babies to barren women by merely rubbing his hands on their bellies. She set off without delay to meet this famous Dibia who was known to have arrived from a distant town to work in the area for a short time. She had a long and tiresome trek before she arrived at the Dibia's house. When she finally got there, she was called in to see the Dibia who was patient enough to listen to her long and pathetic stories of woe. The Dibia expressed profound sympathy for her but confessed that it was unfortunate that she came on a wrong day when he had no child to give to any client. He told her that he had only bad and devilish babies on that day and would not like to give her anything that would break her heart. She persisted to have any breed that was in stock provided it was a human being. She was desperate to have something provided it would be called a human being. He rubbed his hands on her belly and on reaching home; she slept with her husband and the next month she found out that she was pregnant. Her co-wives were not told till after about three months and they found out by themselves that the barren woman was pregnant. Many of them doubted it and gossiped that her stomach was bulging out because she was putting on false weight as a result of much meat and drinks, which their husband secretly gives to her as his favoured wife. After nine months, she was delivered of the baby and it was a male child! This caused a lot of stampede in the community as many came to see the new baby. The boy grew rapidly, both in physique and in intelligence and mischief.

He became rough, stubborn and rude to any one, including his mother and father. The other women in the compound meant nothing to him. He bullied the younger ones and insulted the elders. He took a sharp knife one afternoon and killed all the fowls and goats he found in his mother's house. Thereafter, he went to the other women's houses in the compound and killed all the livestock he found. As if that was not enough, he went into the father's farm and cleared all the yams and crops there. The boy's wanton desire for bloody game increased each new day. He extended his mischievous acts to the neighbours around who began to complain to the Clan Elders. No sooner the elders met to discipline him than he began to behead human beings, killing any one around him. This made many people flee from the village. After killing his parents, he began attacking passers by and some of the old people in the village. No one was able to arrest him, as he appeared too powerful for the young men who gathered to disarm him and banish him from the village. It was discovered that he had very powerful charms that protected him from being attacked by any one. Each person he met would be too weak to attack him because of the powerful charms he was wearing on his waist.

Finally, after the boy had killed all the people in the village, he met one old woman who lived in a little hut in one of the compounds. The old woman in her late 80's was equally equipped with powerful charms she had been wearing for a long time. When the young boy went in to attack the old woman, a very terrible struggle began. He was surprised that she could put up such resistance. The woman waved her charms in a tiny gourd and darkness covered the whole village. The boy, on the other hand, waved his own charms in a bigger gourd   and the whole village got brightened up and the daylight came up. This ding-dong continued until each of them had only one gourd left. They discovered that it was difficult for each of them to surrender. They both clasped each other and immediately turned into two forest creepers intertwined around each other. The old woman's little maid, who was sitting beside them, eating a piece of yam and watching the fight, was changed into an ant carrying a heavy white load. That is why one sees on jungle creepers some little ants carrying some heavy white loads climbing up and down .The two types of charms which the woman and the boy were waving around were responsible for the change we have each day. One was responsible for causing the night and the other for the day. Since they were equally matched, we have the same number of hours of daylight and darkness making one day. The constant way by which the charms were waved became so rhythmic that we have day and night alternating in a constant rhythm as one succeeds the other in an endless continuity.

COMMENTS

The myth sounds like a legend but it is believed that the spirits responsible for Day and Night are equally matched in power. None of the two can overcome the other. There is equal day and equal night in Igbo land. None is longer than the other. The supernatural control of the universe is thus expressed in the myth. The Igbo still believe that there are charms which function in a principle of magic and of reactions of opposing forces. Charms are deeply rooted in the struggle between the mysterious spiritual powers that inhabit the universe. These are symbolically expressed in the charms held by the boy and the old woman. That charm of the old woman was the only mystical force that could match the mysterious powers of the boy. The Igbo believe that Actions and Reactions are Equal and Opposite.

This is another way of expressing the Igbo belief and concept of duality- things go in pairs, there is duality in the universe- Black and White, Long and Short, Male and Female, Darkness and Light, Life and Death.

1.8   Creation of Man
   (Version from Umuopara, Ibeku Umuahia, South Igbo Subculture Area)

Chukwu Okike (Creator God) who is also called *Chineke* made man with Uro (clay). After he had made the world, Chukwu collected some quantity of clay and moulded a figure in the shape of human being. Soon after he had completed the shape of man, Chukwu touched the figure but there was no movement, no speech, no sensitivity, no breath, nothing absolutely! It was just stiff and immovable. Chukwu who is believed to be a master Craftsman felt disappointed. He thought of the next thing to do because he wanted the moulded figure to move about and talk with him. Chukwu had created the animals, plants and trees and other living creatures on earth. All the living creatures were taking commands from Chukwu but could not communicate with him intimately. Chukwu noticed that the figure he moulded with clay would add vibrancy and **beauty** to the created universe if he could be given the strength to move around.

Chukwu therefore breathed into the nostrils of the figure he moulded. There and then the static object began to move, speak and handle things. This pleased Chukwu and he took delight in his work as accomplished.

The figure began to make the environment get new vibrancy and a feeling of fullness. He started to tend the garden, feed some of the animals, clear the footpaths, and mow the lawn. Chukwu decided to call the new creature- **Mma-ndu**- implying the *beauty of life, the essence of life, the dignity of life*. The new creature became the centre of all moving things in the universe and in effect took control of the directing, instructing and naming all the creatures, which Chukwu had made earlier. So humans became the central figure in the created universe and gave new meaning, life, zest and excitement to the living creatures. So life in the universe will be dull, uneventful, and unexciting, without the presence and activity of humans. Life on earth becomes meaningful only when *MMA-NDU* is added to it. When the breath in the *Mma-Ndu* goes off, he turns back to ordinary clay- *Uro*- he becomes ordinary dust from which Chukwu moulded him. It is only when the breath of God is in man that life becomes factual and active.

COMMENTS

The idea of God moulding human life from clay is obviously peculiar to this part of Igbo land. We were convinced after a long discourse that it was not an idea borrowed from the Biblical account of creation. God is often described as *OKPU-ITE-* A Potter – in this part of Igboland. The other view of creation of man was that the first human being was sent down from the sky on the marshy earth surface. The Nri traditions mentioned the sending down of the first man and his wife Namuaku and the other wife Oboli .The notion that the essence of life is the Breath or Spirit, which God puts into humans, is herein underlined. The breath of life- UME-NDU is the real essence of life. If the breath goes off, the human body turns into ordinary dust of clay. So it is with the Spirit-*Nmuo*- if the spirit goes off, life ends.

The essence of MMA-NDU- human being- in Igbo concept of the world is clearly seen in the central position humanity occupies in Igbo Religious and Social Life. African religious belief is **Anthropocentric** not **Theocentric.** The Igbo worship God primarily to preserve man, whom he sees as the Centre of God's creation. Igbo Religious cosmology is basically *Man-centred* not *God-centred*. In fact every moral and ethical rule is enacted to protect man from death and total annihilation and not primarily to honour God per se. All sacrificial rituals are performed to preserve humans on earth. Taboos (*Nso- Ana, Nso Ala,*) and rituals of purification are maintained in order to shield humans from the wrath of angry gods and capricious deities. It is in fact, humans who are given the attention. Laws that do not favour human freedom and activities are described as inhuman. Invariably, the Igbo place high premium on human life and health. This is shown in the names people bear. Some of those names include:

Nduka-aku   Life is more precious than wealth

Ndu bu isi-   Life is the primary concern

Ndukwe   - If life is spared, we can do much

Nduwuba-   Life is the essence of wealth

Ndubueze-   It is life that determines who should be king

Mmaduka - humans are more important

Mmadu akonam (mmadu akolam) - humans should not be in short supply

Mmadu wu uba- Humans are more precious than wealth

Mmadujibeya- Humans are the real preservers of other humans

Mmaduegbuna- may no humans kill me

Mmaduebuka- humans are great

> Mmadubuike- Humans are the main backbone of my strength.

The notion of direct creation of humans by God seems to nullify that of assigning the role to Chi or Eke as the spirits responsible for creation of individual souls and personalities. We might see them as mere guardians of individual psyche and fortune or destiny instead of direct Creators of human life. Probably, the traditional Igbo religious theologian and philosopher do not confuse the issue of roles in his understanding of God and the other major divinities. He may see the divinities as acting on behalf of the Supreme Being- Chukwu or Chineke to whom they are directly responsible.

1.9 Chukwu gives fire to man (Myth from Nkwerre, in the Isu-ama subunit of the South Igbo Subculture Area)

Man has no fire on earth in the distant past. He ate his food raw. When it was cold, he could only warm himself from the rays of the sun, which was the only source of heat then. People often gathered outside their huts to bask themselves in front of the rays of the sun.

The dog is a friendly animal. He is always afraid of cold. He likes to sit close to any member of the family. Most of the time, the dog would travel to many places especially in warm weather during the day. Yet he likes coming home to sit close to someone when it is cold. He likes travelling and would bring home something to his master whenever he sees something like pieces of cloth, bones and pieces of iron. His master likes to send the dog to run some errands for him. So the dog became a constant traveller and a very faithful friend.

On one of his numerous travels, the dog met an old woman who was warming herself by a reddish flame she lit in her room on a very cold harmattan evening. On seeing the reddish flame, the dog in his friendly way went in to greet the woman who welcomed him with smiles. You do not need to book an appointment to visit any one in Igboland and no visitor is excluded. The old woman offered the dog a small stool to sit on. The dog, rather requested to come close to the reddish flame that was producing some warmth and heat that made the room comfortable and cosy. He discarded the stool and sat on bare floor, close to the source of the heat.

He so enjoyed the warmth that he requested the old woman to give him part of the reddish flame to take home to his master.

The friendly old woman gave the dog some glowing reddish charcoal to take home to his master. Since the dog could not hold the hot charcoal by hand, he held it in the mouth. That is why the dog is still panting each time he is running because of the urgency with which he dashed home that night. He did not want the coal to go out or to burn him.

On reaching his master's house, the dog dropped the fire charcoal at a corner and collected some pieces of firewood and set up the fire. He placed his head near the fire and invited other members of the family to come and enjoy the warmth produced by the fire. Thereafter, the man began to boil some yams, roast some meat and cooked some other things with the fire introduced by the dog. That is why today, each time you see the dog, it is close to the fireplace with his head facing the source of fire. Besides, the dog is man's best friend among all the domestic animals.

People came to the man's house to collect some pieces of red-hot charcoal and took them to their own homes to set up the same type of heating instrument they found. Gradually the entire neighbourhood got fire. Since then, the Igbo began to go to their neighbour's houses to collect fire to set up in their homes when they wanted to cook or warm themselves. That is how the people began to go to their neighbours to collect some flames of fire or charcoals. That was before the invention of match -stick. No one allowed the fire to go out. Whenever it went off, there would be some one in whose house others can get some life flame or hot charcoal to set up fire in their own homes. It is a mark of good neighbourliness that the Igbo go to other people's homes to ask for fire or borrow something when in need.

The other version of how fire came into existence was by an accidental striking of a knife on a stone by a farmer who was trying to clear his garden. When his knife struck a stone, flames of fire came up and fell on the dry grass, thereby setting them ablaze. He was able to preserve some woods that were still smothering after the burns. He took it home and thereby began to use it to cook and boil his food. Previously, man ate his food raw and had nothing to keep himself warm in cold season

COMMENTS

The dog is one of the most useful domestic animals in the Igbo world. He serves as a powerful night watchman, and a companion in game hunting.

Dogs suffer a lot of cold during the wet seasons and harmattan and often look for warm place to sit or lie down. The dog spends a lot of its time in the kitchen, either warming itself or waiting for something to fall from the cooking pots for him to eat. He is a very friendly member of the family who tries to play with everyone. The idea of late introduction of fire can be ascertained from the history of the primitive cave man that was initially a migrant traveller. He did not settle down but was moving from place to place. There is a version that states that the dog obtained fire from the Spirit world. He stole it from one of the spirits called

Amadioha – the god responsible for thunder and fire. He stole it and brought it to his master who set it up and began to use it in his cooking, and melting of iron for guns and manufacturing of farming implements. That is why the Amadioha deity has always tried to attack thieves with lightning and thunder to punish those who go about stealing people's property. The Igbo believe that the Amadioha deity strikes only criminals especially thieves with dangerous lightning flames and burns them with fire.

N

IGALA

IDOMA

TIV

EDO

Omabala River

Enugwu-Ezike

Ezza

BENIN

Anambra R.

Ezu River

Nsuka

Aguleri

Ila

Enugwu

Abakaliki

Isele-Ukwu Asaba

Umudioka

Dunukofia

Udi

Agbo

Igbo-Uzo

Onicha

Oka

Akpu-Ajali

Nnewi

Nri

Uburu

Ihiala

Igbo-Ukwu

Afikpo

Ogwashi-Ukwu

Osamara

Okigwe

Abiriba

YAKO

Akoko

Niger River

Olu

Ohafia

Kwale

Ugwuta

Umuahia

Abam

Cross River

URHOBO
ISOKO

Abo

Urashi River

Owere

Enyiogwugwu

Mbaise

Bende

Arochukwu

UMON

Imo River

Aba

Ikwere

IBIBIO

EKOI

P. H.

ANANG

IJO   OGO   NI

Opobo

Bonny

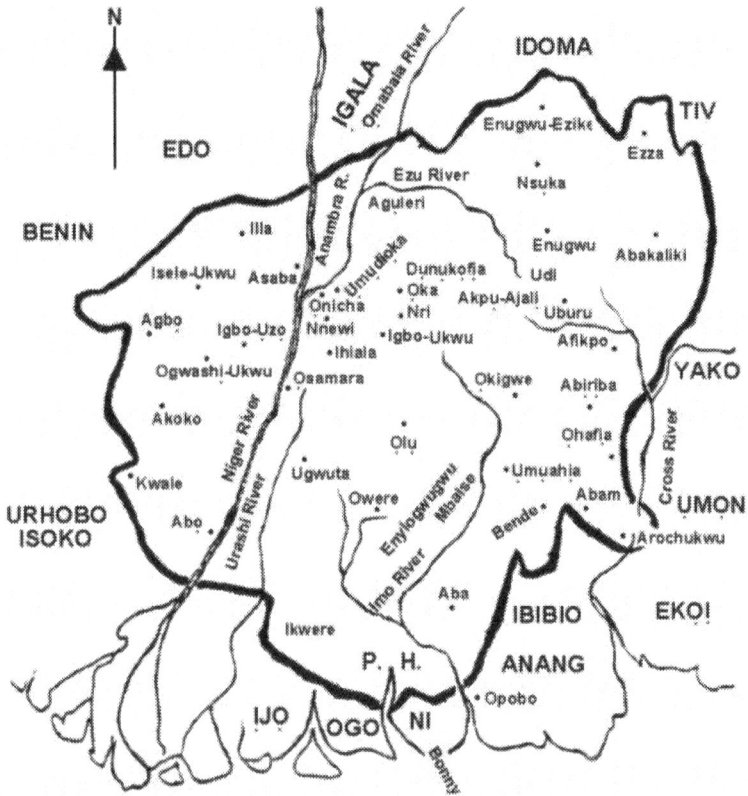

BIGHT OF BENIN

BIGHT OF BIAFRA

GULF OF GUINEA

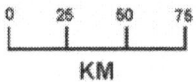

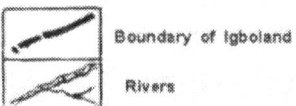

0   25   50   75

KM

MAP OF IGBOLAND IN NIGERIA

Boundary of Igboland

Rivers

CHAPTER TWO
MAN AND FAMILY LIFE

2.1 Origin of Marriage
(Version from Enugu-Ezike, North-Igbo Subculture Area

When Chukwu created the first man, he also gave him a wife directly by himself. The first couple got four male children. After a long time, the couple had a daughter, a very beautiful little girl, whom they called Nwa-oma (a beautiful child, a good child) She was really good-looking and shapely. Her brothers loved her and cared for her very much. She became the baby of the house and everyone admired her for her beauty and good manners. She was not only beautiful in her look but also in character and behaviour. There were no neighbours around and no kids to play with. So the family did not have much to do with outsiders. The four boys and the little girl were the children in the family. Nwa-oma grew up among the four brothers who looked after her and protected here very well.

Although Nwa-oma was the only girl in the family, she was not left to behave anyhow. She was a disciplined girl and her four brothers tried to restrict her from doing certain things. She was not a spoilt child. She was taught domestic chores including cooking and doing the dishes. She accompanied them to the farm and helped in looking after the domestic animals in the home. Although Nwa-oma loved her brothers and parents and lived a normal family life with them, she had also wanted some time to relax and play. As she was growing into a big girl, she demanded to be treated like one and no longer like a baby to be watched and supervised by elder siblings. She needed a little freedom of her own. She wanted her parents and elder brothers to treat her with some measure of respect like a mature girl and not like one who must always take orders from more senior people. She was not allowed to move out freely and explore the neighbourhood.

Nwa-oma was going to the farm one morning with her elder brothers. She saw a group of boys who were playing at the shade of a tree. She did not know that there was another family living in another part of the village. She was excited to see the three boys and one of them caught her attention and she smiled at him. At a point in time, she secretly left her brothers in the farm to join the three boys she saw on their way to the farm. No member of the family knew when she sneaked out and in. On meeting the boys, one of them spoke tenderly to her in a way she had never been all her life. The three brothers treated her in a way that her own brothers had never done before. She enjoyed the change of environment and atmosphere since this was her first time to meet people from outside her own family. The three brothers treated her friendly and she enjoyed their company. She left them after some time and rejoined her brothers at the farm. The next day, she left the farm again and joined the other boys and spent some time with them. Her brothers did not know that Nwa-oma had discovered this family and had been enjoying their company. The third time she visited the boys, she decided to stay and not to return to her family again.

The family was upset when they could not find her. They set up a search party to look for her. Finally they found her in the midst of those boys playing and enjoying some jokes. This annoyed her brothers who struggled to take her home. No amount of persuasion could convince her to follow her brothers home. She said she preferred to stay and spend the rest of her life with the three young men. When her family discovered that it was unnecessary to continue to pressurize her to return with them, they decided that they would go into negotiation with the other family. A peaceful negotiation began and compromise reached.

Nwa-oma's family demanded some compensation. A diviner was consulted and it became clear to both families that Ezechitoke (Chukwu-the Supreme God) has sanctioned the relationship between Nwaoma and one of the three boys she went to live with. The other family has no daughter to give in exchange. So Nwa-oma's family accepted some domestic animals, food items and landed property in exchange in order to validate and regularize her stay in the other family. There and then, a new relationship was established and new covenant enacted. The two families got reconciled and blessed Nwaoma. Friendship and good relationship blossomed between them.

At the beginning, the three boys in the new family began to sleep with Nwa-oma one after the other. Chukwu got angry and warned them that it was wrong. It was only the eldest boy of the three who should have Nwa-oma as his wife and bedmate. The other two brothers left Nwa-oma for their eldest brother. Since then, no two men in Igboland can share a wife together. Girls have from that time been leaving their parents' homes and have found themselves building new homes with their husbands who are not related to them by blood. In Igboland it is the woman who leaves her father's compound to live in another one as a wife and not the man leaving his for the wife's own.

Besides, as a compensation for missing Nwa-oma's services, presence in the family, love, etc, her family accepted the gifts from her new husband's family. It was not a selling price for her but a token gift received as a validation of the relationship. They also presented her with some gifts. This is seen as the origin of the bride price and bride wealth. Unfortunately, when money economy replaced the traditional barter trade, which the people operated in the distant past, gifts, and presents were converted in cash and values changed. Unfortunately, it has been abused to mean charging money as if it is *selling price* on girls being given out for marriage.

COMMENTS

The myth underscores the origin of exogamic form of marriage in Igboland. Incest is not practised in Igbo world. Marriage and sexual attraction do not exist within blood relatives.

i. Women find marriage a fulfilment of life no matter how they are cared for in their fathers' homes.

ii. Discipline should be combined with some measure of freedom and independence as a mark of growth.

iii. The idea of bride price in monetary terms is a late introduction in many parts of Igbo land. It should be seen as a token gift demanded and received not a price for goods sold.

iv. Polyandry is objectionable in Igbo society; and in fact adultery is an abomination! No two men should have sexual relations with a married woman. It is evil and a sin. Adultery can lead to divorce and murder in many parts of Igboland. In the distant past, the culprits were penalized with heavy fine and a ritual of purification performed to cleanse the abomination. In some cases the offended husband demanded some compensation. The practice of concubine was a deviation from divine moral instructions and a late introduction when man lost his age of innocence and sense of purity.

2.2 Man and Woman attract each other
(Version from Abiriba, Cross River Igbo Sub culture Area)

The people of Abiriba in the Cross River Igbo Sub culture area trace the origin of the attraction between a man and a woman to an incident that happened in Isiugwu Ohafia in the distant past. Isiugwu is one of the most popular villages in Ohafia town in the same Cross River Igbo subculture area. While Abiriba excelled in business and commercial enterprises, Ohafia concentrated on education and is one of the Igbo communities that has high rate of literacy. Ohafia has produced many top academics, lawyers and professionals. There are many businessmen and women too.

There was a hunter called Uduma who lived in Isiugwu Ohafia. He used to go out every afternoon in search of animals in the bush. He came by a spring in one of his numerous adventures in the forest. Beautiful rocks and flowers, which attracted Uduma's attention, surrounded the spring and he spent time admiring the beautiful scenery. He later stooped down and drew some quantity of water from the spring to assuage his thirst. Soon after drinking the water he collected with fresh leaves he folded, Uduma fell sick and had stomach trouble.

When he got home Uduma's condition worsened. None of his brothers came to help him in his greatest hour of need. Obasi Di N'elu- (the Supreme God) sent one of the ladies living close to Uduma's house to help him cook his food, wash his clothes and clean his hut. Both hunger and loneliness worsened Uduma's condition before the woman was sent to help him. After eating the food prepared by the woman, Uduma regained some strength and got up. He took the lady to the forest and showed her the spring from which he drank the water that caused his problem. The lady also drank from the spring and the water dried up. Both of them were surprised to see the entire spring dry up within a short space of time. They were so frightened that they decided to go home immediately.

As they were going, Uduma got well on the way. Obasi Di N'elu advised him and the lady to live together to help and support each other. The lady did not go back to her own house but rather accompanied Uduma and ended up living with him. After several weeks, Uduma went to meet his brothers and told them that he would not like to live with them again since they did not help him when he was sick. He would prefer living with the lady whom Obasi Di N'elu advised him to live with.

The brothers did not argue with him. Each decided to build his own separate house and left Uduma with his new found love. Before long, Uduma and the lady were blessed with children. Obasi Di N'elu told them to show the children how to till the ground. This they did and the children became professional farmers instead of hunters.

COMMENTS

Women are known to be very caring and good at nursing sick people. It is believed by the Igbo that relationship between a man and a woman is not primarily romance but a relationship that begins with mutual desire to support each other. When a man marries, there is usually a separation between him and his siblings as each begins to build his own nuclear family.

A man's wife often becomes one's greatest companion in times of hardship. Most brothers would like to come if there is something they can share or grab. The Igbo form of marriage is never embarked upon without the elders ascertaining the opinion of the deities, ancestors and the Supreme Being. It is not an enterprise one embarks upon without the approval of the Divine Beings.

The myth did not set out to explain the origin of marriage but ended up with the cohabitation of man and woman. Probably that was the original state of marriage before money was introduced. It is a bit difficult to assess if traditional marriage in Igboland started that way. Marriage built on mutual love and trust lasts longer than anything built on falsehood. One good turn deserves another. No single person is complete as a full human being. Both man and woman find fulfilment in each other's company.

2.3 Women and Menstruation
(From Abiriba and Ohafia, Cross River Igbo Sub Culture Area)

At the beginning of time when human beings were created, man was very powerful. He looked stronger than woman and did many hard jobs. He was so powerful that Chukwu felt that a regular loss of blood each month would help to control man's excess energy. The loss of blood was to curtail man's excess energy and keep him from going around doing many of the hard things he was fond of doing. Chukwu decided that the blood would be going out from man's body through his genitals. That time, human genitalia were located inside the armpits. The blood that flowed out was regarded as sacred and therefore should be kept away from any human beings, particularly women. Chukwu did not want the woman to suffer any other loss of blood since at labour she experiences a lot of pain and great loss of blood. Further loss would really be unfair to her health and energy. However, he warned the woman not to go close to the man during that painful period of monthly bleeding experience. It was indeed a period of agony for the man and a time Chukwu wanted man to relax and experience a sense of vulnerability as a human being created by God himself. It was a sort of disciplinary device by God to humble the proud and strong man who boasts too much of his prowess and energy.

An inquisitive woman called Ugwuaku visited the man one of the evenings when the man was in serious pain. The man, whose name was Ajula (Don't Ask) was sitting near his hut in severe pains. Ugwuaku was really worried when she saw Ajula in pains and felt she could help him relieve his pains. She wanted to know what the problem was. Although she was trying to show sympathy, Ugwuaku was a very curious and overbearing personality who wanted to know about everything. She wanted to know the source or cause of Ajula's pains.

The man refused to tell her the very spot of the body where the pains were located. She noticed some blood gushing out from Ajula'a armpit. The man was struggling in vain to clean up the part of the body that had been stained by the blood. Ajula refused to allow Ugwuaku to see the spot from where the blood was flowing out. During the long period of argument, Ajula did not know when he raised his hand to scratch his head. On raising the arm, Ugwuaku's eyes went straight to the armpit from where the blood was flowing out. Ajula was embarrassed and felt completely ashamed of himself having allowed the inquisitive woman to see his genitals. This also annoyed Chukwu who had earlier warned women not to go close to men when they are in that state of pain caused by their monthly loss of blood.

Chukwu immediately punished Ugwuaku by transferring the monthly loss of blood with its pains to her. Ajula was relieved of the agony and thenceforth, the woman began to have monthly loss of blood, in addition to the pains at childbirth. Furthermore, Chukwu transferred human genitalia to the lower limbs to hide them from the immediate and open glance of human eyes. Previously, the genitalia were located at the armpits and that is why there are some strands of pubic hairs still growing in the armpits. It is a taboo to fiddle or tickle a man or woman at the armpits as it is seen as sexual harassment in Igbo society. Chukwu punished women with the severe rebuke not to allow a man to touch or come close to them during the period of monthly loss of blood. Thereafter, women began to hide themselves whenever they begin to experience that severe pain and flow of blood. They were banned from making public appearances, fetching water from public streams, cooking the food for their husbands, coming out to welcome visitors in the lounge. They were from that day warned never to initiate any discussion on sex or show open interest in it. They must learn to repress and hide their feelings and never show they enjoy it. Any woman in Igboland who shows open interest in sex is either regarded as a whore, abnormal or wayward. They therefore learnt to pretend about it and feel shy whenever men mention sex.

COMMENTS

Human sufferings in the world are explained as results of gross disobedience to the rules and instructions given by the Supreme Being. Women are particularly pointed out as being the chief culprits. Man's misfortune and hardship came as a result of his wife's wilful disobedience to Divine Instructions. This is however, a common explanation of misfortune in a male-dominated society.

The Igbo frown at children or young people being too inquisitive or curious over any issue. Ugwuaku's insistence on seeing the source of the blood led to the transference of the problem to her. It is not a virtue in Igbo society to be too inquisitive especially in matter elders do not want the young people to have detailed information about. Many taboos about female menstruation might be based on fear and superstition that women should not come out in public at that time. Life is deeply associated with blood and loss of blood is seen as loss of life. Women are considered dirty, impure, source of danger and death during the period of menstruation and must hide from public view. They undergo ritual purification if they come out in public or touch any food items that elders may eat.

Women are expected to subdue their interest in sex and should not show openly that they enjoy it even with their husbands. That traditional inhibition has been the basis of ethical law in Igbo society, which at times has the danger of double morality. It is normal for a man to commit adultery but a crime for a woman. A man caught may be asked to pay a fine but the woman may be divorced or stoned to death!

2.4   World Population Increases
(From Abba Njikoka, Northwest Igbo Subculture Area)

Chukwu lived in the sky above with a man and a woman in the distant past. No one lived on the earth surface then. The creator Chukwu whose other name was *Ugama* lived close to the man and his wife. The three had lovely fellowship although at times Chukwu kept his own distance and private programme to run his universe. The woman called *Ojiri Uka Gba Ama*- (one who talks a lot, who indulges in frivolous tales.) was a great nuisance and talebearer as her name implies. She was talker thief and could scarcely hold her tongue. She and her quiet and gentle husband had two children - a boy and a pretty girl.

The Creator- Ugama- put this woman in a basket with her son and daughter. He put in some large quantity of food and drinks for them- including maize, yam, cassava, sugar cane, etc and lowered them in a well-knit basket to the earth. The family planted a garden on earth and this flourished and produced large quantity of food.

Ojiri Uka Gba Ama lived happily with her two children on earth and enjoyed the bounty of the proceeds from their farm. She, however, began to wonder what would happen to their large estate and property if they died, as their number was still three. The husband was not there with them. She as a schemer she was, insisted that her son should have children. The son asked how possible that would be since they had no other family living close to them. She suggested that the son should raise children with her only daughter (who was the boy's sister). This shocked the boy who refused to comply with the idea. The mother's influence and overbearing personality eventually prevailed. The boy discovered that he could not get his mother to change her mind on this plan. He eventually gave in and went in to his sister with whom he raised children. When they grew in number, some of them deserted the original home and founded other estates where they established their own homesteads. When the original three people died, the offspring could no longer recognise one another or identify each other as coming from the same close blood relations. They thus began to marry one another and thenceforth, the population began to increase and people began to spread to many unoccupied areas of the earth. Nothing was heard about their father who remained behind with Chukwu – Ugama- after the woman and her two children were sent down.

COMMENTS

This is very usual, as it does not circulate in many parts of Igbo territory. Nothing is said about the father who was not sent down with the wife and two children. It is understood that the early people who lived on earth were so few that endogamy was practised. It was long after the increase in the world population that people decided to marry from far places. In some Igbo societies, however, first cousins are encouraged to marry in order to preserve the purity of their stock as well as to preserve inheritance. Many societies who inherit through the mother's line would prefer endogamous marriage to exogamy. The fact that few people lived on earth at the beginning of the world is hereby illustrated

Furthermore, mothers are known to be very much concerned about the continuity of their lineage If a woman does not have a male child, she is tempted to get a wife or a maid for her husband to raise a male issue for her to continue her own lineage. This is particularly true where the woman is rich and has no male issue or no child at all. Mothers encourage their children to marry early enough to enable them get offspring. A mother's influence on marriage and procreation is hereby underscored.

2.5   Human Beings filled up the Surface of the Earth
(From Eha- Alumona, Nsukka, North Igbo Subculture Area)

There was a time in Igbo world, when population was very small. A handful of people lived in large expanse of land especially in Nsukka area where there was large landmass. In Eha- Alumona, for instance, the number of people was very small. A few adult men were known to live in the town. The number of women was also small, although it was a little higher than that of men.   There were absolutely very few youths and children. It gave the elders of the community a very big concern as many of them were dying out and the rate of replacement was very slow.

A very wise man called Eze-Nwa –Enwe- arrived in Eha- Alumona on the invitation of the elders of the town and clan heads to advise them on what to do to increase their population.   The man Eze-Nwa-Enwe was a native doctor and a traditional medicine man from a distant place. He was worried that the big town was in danger of extinction, as its population was not growing at all. A particular village had only two adults living in it. The elders sought Eze-Nwa-Enwe's advice. He told them he would meet Ezechitoke (the Supreme God) on their behalf and obtain suggestion on how to solve their problem and establish the cult of **Abalaeshu** for them.

Eze-Nwa-Enwe brought a monkey (enwe), rat (ntu- ala in Nsukka dialect) and used both of them in a ritual sacrifice to the Ezechitoke (Supreme God). He later cut the two animals into two pieces each. He made holes and inserted the one half of the monkey and a half of the rat into the holes and covered them with sand. He made one pair represent a female and the other a male part. After a few days, the covered parts buried in the two holes began to grow up into a structure like that of an anthill. Thereafter, the number of people in the town began to increase, as the anthill grows daily. The rat was used because it has a very high fertility rate and increases rapidly in the bush that surrounds the town.

The monkey was also used by the medicine man because of its ability to live very long. It does not die young as many monkeys in the bush live to a very ripe old age. The rate of human reproduction became as rapid as that of a rat and on the other hand, the life span of the people living in Eha- Alumona became as long as that of a monkey. So rapid rate of procreation combined with longevity made the population of the earth increase and many began to look for spaces elsewhere to live as the existing land mass was getting too congested. People were no longer dying young and more children were being born in the various communities.

COMMENTS

Eha- Alumona is one of the most highly populated towns in Nsukka. Today, if any one has a high reproductive capacity in the town, he is called a rat. Women who have as many as ten children are described as breeding like rats. The old people who are still waxing strong as they live are described as Enwe – i.e. monkey. The high population density of this town is attributable to the high rate of production and low death rate. The Igbo pay high premium on long life and possession of many children. Both are regarded as very important marks of blessings from the Supreme God. Most sacrificial rites are performed to have children and to preserve life to a ripe old age.

The desire to have children is a very strong one in Igbo society. It is one of the primary aims of marriage. Most sexual acts were aimed at raising offspring, not necessarily for the fun of it. That is why a woman often ignores relationship with her husband and concentrates on training and caring for her children. Childcare and maintenance is the primary concern of the mother. When a woman gets less interested in sexual acts because of the great burden of looking after her numerous children, the husband may be encouraged or tempted to have another wife with whom he can have sex whenever he needed it. It is one of the reasons for polygamy and probably what people may frown at as Child Marriage. A man of fifty whose wives are passed the age of childbearing and have lost interest in sexual acts may choose to marry younger ones who may be of the same age with his daughters. This looks absurd but it is the moral way to check promiscuity among men and to allow women opportunity to look after their kids.

2.6   CIRCUMCISION IN IGBO SOCIETY
(Version from Isu- Ama subunit of South Igbo Sub Culture Area)

A long time ago, man and woman walked about naked. None was ashamed or afraid of the other. The beautiful figure and strong masculine muscles of a man would show him a strong personality while woman's shapely figure made her look beautiful. It was reported that one day, the woman saw her husband's erect penis and got frightened. It was her first time to see it in that position. Usually when they sleep in the night to make children, none of them would look at each other's genitals or discuss it. So that casual glance at the erect penis on that fateful afternoon, gave the woman a shock of life. She thought that her husband had bought it as a new weapon to punish her or flog her. She regarded it as a very strong whip and an instrument of punishment because the size was much bigger and longer that what she knew it to be. She began to think of what to do to protect herself from being harmed by her husband in case he got up one day to flog her with it.

She consulted a diviner to seek advice on what to do. On her way, the woman met the Agwu Deity- the patron deity of medicine, which at times acts in a vicious, and rash way and can strike people mad. The deity advised her to cut off the organ slightly so that it would not be active to harm her at any time.

One evening, the man felt asleep. His wife lay beside him. When she discovered that her husband was already fast asleep, she brought out a sharp knife, which she had been hiding since she got the advice from the Agwu deity. She placed the sharp knife on the relaxed penis to cut off part of it. She could not complete the work but succeeded in removing the foreskin that covers the penis. The man woke up in pain with blood everywhere in the room. She began to cry thinking that the man would die. She turned round to apply first aid to the husband who was in severe pain. She applied several ointments including oil, salve, and cream on the wound. After some days the cut was healed. The woman apologised to her husband and promised not to harm him again. She was afraid that the man would die and the thought of it made her feel guilty the more. Later after the wound had healed, the woman looked at the scar at the tip of the penis and liked the new shape of the penis. She confessed that it looked more beautiful than it was previously, but the man did not believe her. In order to convince him of her sincerity, the woman began to fondle the husband's genital which she thought was a dangerous weapon before. Since that time, women have stopped fearing their husbands and could walk in front of them boldly having discovered that the organ they thought was an instrument of punishment was really not dangerous. That is why women are known to be beautiful circumcisers and artists in Igboland.

After the wound had been healed, the woman began to envy the beauty of the shape of her husband's penis. It looked more beautiful than it was previously. She decided to do something on herself to make her own genitals as beautiful as that of her husband. This time she decided to go to meet Chukwu (the Supreme God) directly. One of the agents at the Chukwu's gate refused her entry. She turned back in anger. On getting home, when her husband was at the back garden doing some work, the woman picked up a sharp knife again to see if she could find similar organ inside her genitals to cut it as beautiful as she did that of her husband. She could not see any organ as long as her husband's own in her private part. She noticed a small object that looked like her husband's penis- her clitoris. She decided to make it look as beautiful as that of her husband but was disappointed that the knife reduced the size to a very small shape. A lot of blood gushed out and she had painful experience. The wound was not healed till after several days. Her husband was really sad when he came in and saw her in a pool of blood. He also helped to nurse her till the wound was healed. The clitoris was mutilated instead and that did not really please her.

After Izu-Ano (four Igbo weeks) i.e. sixteen days, the woman's wound was completely healed. She took her husband's penis an inserted it into herself to ascertain if the wound had been completely healed. The women from that day started cutting off part of their clitoris to make sure that it looked like their husbands' organs.

COMMENTS

What turned out to be a very important ritual practice had its origin in a very bizarre way. Women are known to be beautiful artists and makers of aesthetic marks and prints on human body. Many traditional circumcisers are women and it is believed that it is not as painful as circumcision made by men. It is not a mark of test of strength and maturity in men as it may be in some other communities. In other words, it is not an initiation rite in Igbo society. The original act was done in old age but today it is a rite that takes place eight days after the birth of a male child. It may be due to the pains that circumcision causes that the Igbo changed the time of its performance on males on the eighth day of a male child's birth.

The traditional Igbo women practised circumcision of women. The ritual cannot be called circumcision per se but *cliteridectomy*- mutilation of the clitoris. Probably, it was performed on girls for reasons other than aesthetics. Some suggested that it was performed to check women from being easily excited and thus end up in prostitution and waywardness.

This reason has no mythical foundation. Probably it could be because it was performed on male children and must also be arried out on females too. No matter the reason, the C.MS. Christian Missionaries discouraged the ritual as being savage and brutal for purely medical reasons. The Igbo have very high premium on continence and sexual purity. Many ethnographers and Igbo Cultural Anthropologists and Historians have suggested that the Igbo practice of performing the rite of circumcision on male children on the eighth day of birth gives credence to the theory of Igbo links with the Jews. This is yet to be confirmed or validated with authentic ethnographic data.

2.7   MATRILINEAL INHERITANCE
(From Anofia Afikpo, Northeast Igbo Subculture Area)

A rich man in Anofia had a sister who was married to a man in another village. The rich man had four wives and many children from them. He loved one of the wives more than the rest and this was a cause of quarrel among the co-wives. In spite of occasional secret favour the man showed to his most beloved wife, he used to give all of them their rights and provided them with food and money as well as farm lands in such a way that none of them lacked care and maintenance.

The rich man killed a young man in the bush when his gun made an accidental discharge on a day he and his friends went to hunt some games. He was a very popular hunter and people knew him as a skilful marksman. The gods of Anofia had earlier decreed that the punishment for such offence was the death of the man who fired the shot. Although it was no murder, the offence merited capital punishment. The offender was, in addition, expected to provide a replacement to the bereaved family. The elders in the village tried the case and found the rich man guilty of homicide, which deserved capital punishment.

A day was set for the man to face the firing squad. The system was quite straightforward. He could provide a substitute to face the firing squared on his behalf or face it himself. Secondly, only one shot would be fired. If it kills the man, it is assumed that justice has been done. If the shot misses him, that ends the matter. The man made overtures to get somebody to face the firing squad on his behalf.

He approached his first wife- Lolo- who had five boys to allow one of the boys to die on his behalf. The wife was so angry that she accused the man of partiality and hatred for her own nuclear family particularly her sons. She refused to allow any of her sons to die for their father. Failing to get the support of his first wife, the man contacted his second wife who had four boys. She refused too. The third wife did not even show any interest and asked the man to go and die as it was his sin of partiality that led him to that trouble. None of the three wives allowed their sons to die for their father. Hoping that the youngest wife whom he loved very much would allow one of her three sons to stand in for him, he felt completed devastated when she burst out in anger that she would not allow her own sons who were much younger than the other wives' sons to die for their father. This upset the man to a point of distress that none of his wives and their sons showed interest in his life.

The rich man's only sister married in the next village came to see him a day before the appointed date for the execution. She was so worried about the thought of her only brother being killed for such offence. When she heard that her brother's wives refused to allow any of their sons to die for their father, the woman jumped up on the spot and told the brother that she would allow her only son to die for his uncle. She made the offer in desperation and felt that it was the only way to save her brother from death. Her offer of her son was considered a huge sacrifice on her part.

The entire community gathered at the community square on the morning of the execution. The young man had come out prepared to die for his uncle. There was tension and anxiety all over the place. Many were perplexed that their respected Ada – noble daughter- should make such a sacrifice to redeem her brother. The young man stood on the gallows and a marksman was asked to fire a shot at him. The shot missed the man and he was instantly declared free. The rule was that if the bullet did not get him down, the case was over but if he died, the man would still provide a substitute to the family of the man who was killed in the accident.

When the young man was not killed, the sympathisers and other friends jumped up in excitement. The man, himself was overwhelmed. His sister was mad with joy. There was uproar everywhere in the entire Anofia. The man mounted the platform in the presence of the large crowd and the community leaders and made a proclamation. He stood up in excitement and joy and publicly announced that his sister's son- his nephew, would from that day, inherit his rich assets. None of his sons who were stopped by their mothers to die for him would inherit his property. He thus, disinherited his own sons and their mothers. Thus inheritance began to pass on through the female line which was based on the principle of one good turn deserves another. It was the talk of the town for many years. Although his nephew did not pack his things to live in his compound, the young man took over the management of his uncle's property from that day as the heir apparent. When his uncle died eventually, he moved into the compound to take over the assets.

COMMENTS

Inheritance through the male line is the common tradition in many parts of Igboland except in places like Ohafia and Abriba and Ehugbo where matrilineal system operates.

The myth explains the unusual love ties and friendship and spirit of confidence that normally exists between a man and his nephew through his sister's side. It explains again the emotional love between a man and his sister. It tries to show why **Umuada-(Umuokpu)-** daughters who have married - are highly respected in their fathers' compounds. They are willing to make any sacrifice for the peace and progress of their maiden homes. Usually many men in Igbo land reposed more confidence in their sisters than in their wives. So also many women love their brothers more than they love their husbands. We are not justifying the practice but it seems to be the way the Igbo see relationships in their socio-religious world. A woman takes more pride in her brother's success than in that of her husband, especially if it is a polygamous marriage.

The myth underscores the rivalry and suspicion in polygamous marriage. None of the wives, even the most favoured, believed that the man's life was precious to be saved. None of the wives could make the type of sacrifice the man's sister made.

The myth again gives backing to the importance and influence to the role of **UMU-ADA (Umu- Okpu**) married daughters in their father's compound. Their sacred role as peacemakers, impartial judges, and altruistic benefactors can be seen in this myth. No woman thinks that her contribution for the progress of her father's home and family would ever be too much. They can go to any length to sacrifice for the peace and progress of their fathers' houses from their matrimonial home. Besides the political and sacred role of *Umu-Ada (Umu-okpu)* in their maiden home is validated by their love and commitment to the good of the family. They are authority figures in their maiden homes, and enjoy the respect of all including their senior siblings. In old age, many of them are brought back home to adjudicate in any case that defies the court of elders.

Often they are taken back to their maiden home for burial when they die. It is important to state the sacred roles of these married daughters in their fathers' compounds. Many of them can overdo it and cause problems among their brothers.

2.8   Udala Tree and the Gift of Children, (From Abatete, Idemmili, And Northwest Igbo Subculture Area)

In Abatete, the Udala (Udara) tree is a sacred tree planted by Chukwu himself. It is so in many parts of Igbo world. The Earth Goddess (Ana, Ani, Ala) nourishes this beautiful evergreen tree that does not shed its leaves. It produces beautiful fruits that attract many people, particularly children. No one is allowed to climb the tree to pluck the fruit. No one harvests it for sale as an individual does usually not own it, no matter how close a tree may be to a man's house or located in his garden. It is usually regarded as the tree that belongs to the gods and should be accessible to the use of any humans around.   Any one passing through Udala tree can pick its fruit if it falls .It is seen as a mark of favour or blessing from the gods.

Chukwu (Supreme God) sent the Udala trees to Ezeogu, the ancestral founding father of the Abatete people when his wife had been barren for a long time. Chukwu told Ezeogu in a dream to go to the Udala tree in his compound to pick some fruit that had fallen from it. When Ezeogu got up from the sleep, he walked straight to the Udala tree and picked some fruits that had fallen. In another development, Chukwu asked Ezeogu to pick as many as he could and that the number of fruits of Udala he picked would be the number of children his wife would have. He was also asked to distribute the fruit among the children in the village whom he would meet on his way as they come to look for some fruits. This he did without quibble. His wife became pregnant and soon gave birth to the first son. She became pregnant again and had a boy. This continued till Ezeogu and his wife got eight sons. Later they adopted another son whom they picked up near the Udala tree and made him one of their sons. Thus they had nine sons. The nine sons used to gather under the shade of the big Udala tree in front of Ezeogu's house. It became a playground for them. This attracted other children from the community who gathered there to wait for the fruit to fall as they joke and play around. That is why today, the Udala tree attracts a lot of children and forms a traditional playground for them especially when it has ripe fruits on it.

The nine children of Ezeogu became the ancestors of the nine villages that make up Abatete town. The name of the town is **MBA – ITEGHETE**- (Nine Towns). It was the Colonial administrators and Christian Missionaries that changed it to Abatete, which sounded easier for them to pronounce.

COMMENTS

The myth underscores the essence of children as gift from God.

    i. The gods may bless any good man who is kind and generous with numerous children.

    ii. Today, Udala is normally seen as a symbol of childbirth and barren women are usually asked to go and dance with children under Udala Tree.

    iii. Udala tree attracts children and any person who arrives at the time a fruit falls is regarded as a lucky being who is loved by the gods.

    iv. Children are warned not to go the Udala tree when it is either too late or early in the morning or midday because some dangerous and mischievous spirits go around that time to hunt for children to kill. Evil spirits that hate children usually go to the Udala tree to look for those to attack.

v. Some interpreters or translators of Igbo language wrongly call the Udala *an Apple* or Fig Tree. It seems to be tropical tree that does not grow in temperate climate and therefore does not still have an appropriate English equivalent.

CHAPTER THREE
GOD AND MAN IN PERSONAL
RELATIONSHIP AND ENCOUNTER

3.1   Chukwu withdraws to the Sky above
(Version from Abiriba, Cross River Igbo Subculture Area)

Man and God lived very close to each other in prehistoric times- *mmadu na Obasi Di N'elu bi nso na oge gbo*-gbo. They lived like close friends, talked freely to each other and man had no problems in getting things off his friend – God.

Man's basic food then was yam, which he normally pounded into *foo-foo-utara ji, nni ji.* Other food crops included cocoyam, maize, three-leafed yam (una), pineapple, bitter leaf that he enjoyed as a regular vegetable for his pounded yam delicacy. The man's wife was an expert in pounding her husband's yam into his foo-foo. She took time to prepare this meal for her husband each day. She had a very deep mortar and a long pestle. The pounding usually took a long time and each time, it produced some unpleasant noise that disturbed Chukwu who was their closest neighbour.

Chukwu, being the type of gentleman he was, felt that he would not like to quarrel with his friend and his wife. He therefore, withdrew from the sight of man and his wife and decided to go and live far from them where their noise would no longer disturb him. He did this while the man and his wife were asleep. So when they got up, they could not find him after searching for him for a long time, Chukwu went up and covered himself with white clouds, which hid him from man's sight.

When eventually they looked up, the man and his wife noticed that Chukwu their friend had gone to live beyond the clouds and they began to cry: *O laghila! O laghila! O laghila-! Oh he is gone! O he is gone! O he is gone!* From that day, each time the man and his wife wanted to talk to Chukwu, they had to look upwards to the Sky. Thenceforth, humans began to look for God upwards! That is why the Igbo call God – Obasi Di N'elu- God who lives above!

Version from Mbano, Isu-ama Subunit of South Igbo Subculture Area

There was a time when Igwe (Sky) was very close to Ala- the Earth. Man was living on the earth and he could draw his food from the sky and pick up anything he wanted from above as well as dig out food and fruits from the soil. So he had easy reach to both the earth and sky. He had enough food and could have anything without difficulty. He was talking with Chukwu easily as a human can talk to his next-door neighbour. He held very many discussions and chats with Chukwu in the cool of the evenings. It was a period of bliss and joy for man and woman then living on the earth.

One unfortunate incident happened one afternoon. Chukwu was having a quiet rest in the day. A greedy woman, who did not wash her hands after eating a meal of pounded yam, touched the 'face of the sky' while trying to draw more food for her family. This act amounted to profanation of the sacred and purity of the face of the Supreme Deity who felt angry about that act of insubordination and carelessness. Chukwu, there and then decided to move higher up to avoid being desecrated by humans who would carelessly stroll into his chambers. Consequently, the sky moved up higher than where human hands can reach easily. Man also lost the opportunity to talk to Chukwu directly as he was doing before. That was the beginning of Chukwu's new home far above man's reach.

Version from Ezihe, Mbano Isu-ama Subunit South -Igbo Subculture Area

Chukwu lived very close to man in the distant past. Humans could talk to him and with him easily. He enjoyed talking with man at the cool of the evening. There was no protocol in going to him. People were really enjoying his presence as a Big Chief or Big Judge who could settle their cases whenever people had misunderstanding.

Humans began to take their cases to Chukwu for adjudication. Most of the time, even minor disputes over a piece of land to plant vegetable, were taken to Chukwu to settle. Women who had misunderstanding in the market or at the stream would take their cases to Chukwu for settlement. It became so frequent that Chukwu felt that humans were distracting his attention from running the bigger business of controlling the universe. He felt that some agents could be delegated to look into minor cases and quarrels which humans encounter as they live together in the world. Thus Chukwu disappeared to a higher level where man would not easily reach him any longer. He then sent some of his senior agents to the world to take care of every department of human life-agriculture, marriage, childbirth, market, health, etc. Any one, who needs anything to be discussed or has a problem to sort out in any area of life, will then consult Chukwu's minister in charge of that department. That minister would in turn go to Chukwu on behalf of the person who came for consultation. Thus the idea of minor gods and major intermediary deities began. The Supreme Being from that day became the last port of call when other deities or agents had failed man.

The other version said that a woman who lost her only son used to cry early morning every day. Her constant crying and wailing disturbed Chukwu's quiet time. This continued disturbance by the woman's early morning cry made Chukwu move up his abode where humans would not disturb him any longer.

Thus humans found it difficult to reach Chukwu's home with minor problems that could be handled by the agents of Chukwu who lived around.

COMMENTS

This myth tries to explain the distance separating the Supreme Being and humans in the world. The distance is understood to be in morality, holiness, purity, greatness and power. It is not in terms of personal relationship and care. It explains the relationship between societal structure where the Head of the Clan is close to his subjects but not in terms of living in the same hut with them. God lives **above** yet he is **immanent**. He is not an absentee Landlord or King. He could be reached or approached any time and any place. His presence is never distant from his people. That is why the Igbo have no effigy or image of Chukwu to represent him as if he is not close to them. There are images of other deities and gods, but none of Chukwu who is known to be everywhere at anytime. He is ubiquitous and omnipresent as well as omniscient. The Igbo express this view in personal names like

Chukwuno-nso	- God is near
Chukwudi	- God is there; there is God
Chinedu	- God leads, God is leading me,
Chukwuebuka	- God is so big
Munachiso	- I am with God or God is following me
Elemchukwu	- I am looking unto God; I wait upon God

No matter what happens, the name Chukwu is on the lips of an Igbo person. Some foreign interpreters of African Traditional Religion and Culture had erroneously explained this myth to imply God's **remoteness and withdrawal from man**. Hence they used some pejorative terms to describe the African Concept of God as **Deus Remotus, (-the Remote God), Deus Otiosus, (the Withdrawn God) Deus Absconditus, etc.** God is neither withdrawn nor absent from the Igbo Traditional Theology and Concept of the Deity.

Women have been projected in all the versions of the myths as the source and cause of God's reason for going a bit far from his close home with men. It may be the Igbo man's own theological presentation of the Loss of Edenic bliss. But we must note that in a male-dominated cult, it is the woman who is the scapegoat for every misfortune.

Every society has got its own version of the Fall of Man and this may probably stand as a genre of that story. The fall tried to explain man's loss of special privilege from the hand of God. Just as the Biblical Adam lost the bliss of the Garden of Eden, man in Igbo cosmology lost the chance to live closer to God, which he enjoyed in his age of innocence and purity. Living close to a big and popular nobles is regarded by the Igbo as a mark of success or an opportunity to get rich – e.g. the Igbo would say **Adighi Ukwu n' Eze A baa uba**- *Living close or supporting the King brings wealth.* It has its own problems too. Hence the saying- *Mbidebe Ogaranya* nwere ike buru *uru ma o bu oghom*- Living close to the rich brings either gain or a huge loss.

3.2   Chukwu leaves Awo-Omama for Arochukwu
(Version from Awo- Omama in the South Igbo Subculture Area)

Chukwu- Abiama is a female deity commonly known and addressed as Nne- Anyi (**Our Mother**) in Awo-*Omama* community. She was the Supreme Deity of the community. Her abode was in a deep valley in the part of the town called **Obibi.** This shrine is still regarded as the old home of the Supreme God in the whole universe.

The people of *Awo-Omama* used to consult **Chukwu- Abiama** (the **All- Wise and Benevolent Deity**) for fortune telling and other needs especially healing and protection from charms and evil spirits. She was highly respected and drew some clients from many other neighbouring communities. Its cult was a thriving one and had many priests at its shrine. Her fame spread far and wide all Igbo known world.

One day, a very intelligent woman set out early morning to test the Chukwu- *Abiama's* worldwide acclaimed wisdom and intelligence. The woman was really envious of the fame Chukwu-Abiama that has attracted a lot of people to revere and worship her as a powerful and gracious deity. She felt that the female deity was just a woman like her and should not be accorded such fame and respect. She was, therefore, bent on finding a way to ridicule Chukwu-Abiama and expose her to the world as a deity that does not deserve the type of popularity she had. She wanted, in other words, to draw attention to herself as an intelligent sage who could be trusted by people for solution to their problems.

The woman hid her kitchen knife somewhere in her house. She decided to go to Chukwu-Abiama, pretending to be looking for her missing knife. She went to consult the deity to help her trace the whereabouts of her 'missing knife'. On getting to the shrine of Chukwu-Abiama, the woman requested the deity to detect the culprit. The deity in her wisdom and spiritual insight discovered the woman's tricks and intrigue and got angry with her. As a benevolent deity, Chukwu-Abiama did not punish her but just reprimanded her for her lies and jealousy. In anger, the deity said, **Nke a abughi ihe m ga-ahu ebea** (this is not what I would be seeing in this place – meaning she would not tolerate people's ingratitude and desecration of her divine authority and purity). She decided to move out from her grove in Awo-Omama to a more secure place where she would be able to have space and convenience to serve her numerous clients and worshippers. Sequel to that, she decided to change her gender from female to male, since it is not easy for women to respect a deity of their own gender. Women in general tend to respect the Supreme God whom they see as a male deity- probably an expression of Oedipus complex and Electra- complex of Greek Mythology in Igbo worldview.

The people of Awo-omama got angry with the jealous woman who provoked the deity to anger. But it was too late for them to appease the angry Chukwu-Abiama who had decided to leave the area. The most convenient place located by Chukwu- Abiama was Arochukwu where there was a very big grove. The Aro people were very glad to welcome her and offered her their most generous hospitality, traditional to Igbo people. After the deity had settled in the town, she told the people that she was no longer a female deity but male. He was to be called Ibinu Ukpabi and that he would appropriate the people as his children. So the town should change its name to **Aro Chukwu** and they should see themselves as **UMU-CHUKWU** (The *Children of God) The* Aro took advantage of their new position and have since then called themselves Umu-Chukwu, Okigbo- (Greater than Igbo) and *Bekee Mbu* (The First Europeans! - indirect acceptance of European superiority to the Black Africans!) They instigated inter-village wars from which captives were sold to the Aros as slaves. They claimed special relationship with the Chukwu and paraded themselves as the people who own and worship the Supreme Creator of Heaven and Earth. They went around inviting the whole Igbo world to come to their Chukwu for solution to all their problems. They used this trick to lure people into believing that their Ibin Ukpabi was the God who made Heaven and Earth and Arochukwu is his earthly home. People were manipulated to go and eventually this turned out to be an organised fraud that led to slave trade that destroyed Igbo economy and history. The colonial administrators who saw the corruption and manipulation of this cult destroyed it in 1910. Although the fame of the Ibinu Ukpabi spread through out the Igbo world, no Aro would tell a fellow Aro man that Ibini Ukpabi was a true Supreme Being. They only used it as an economic strategy to extort money and slaves from the world around. There is a common slogan among the Igbo that no Aro tells a fellow Aro that Ibin Ukpabi has enquired about him- implying that no Aro plays the Ibin Ukpabi tricks on a fellow Aro person who knows that it is fraudulent and false. They sent out secret emissaries to every part of Igbo world to gather information for the Ibinu Ukpabi Oracular services to every one in need. Thus the Aro settlements are found everywhere in Igboland. They were agents of the Chukwu of Arochukwu who were out encouraging people with problems to go on pilgrimage to the Chukwu Deity for solution.

COMMENTS

The myth is complex in a way. It tries to explain the origin of the Ibin Ukpabi- the Oracular Deity of Arochukwu which was not originally there in existence in Aro Mythology and which is not known in Aro Chukwu as the Patron Deity of the Aros but a sort of Commercial Project - **Ubi Aro**- of a few villages that operated it. It was an economic project owned and operated by a few villages in Aro Chukwu. This was the reason no Aro can trick a fellow Aro to the shrine for any material extortion. No Aro would ask a fellow Aro to go to the Ibin Ukpabi for a solution of his problem because they knew it was fake and mere trickery.

Shrewd Aro traders exploited the Igbo hinterland during the heyday of the notorious Slave Trade by extensively using the presence of Ibin Ukpabi in Arochukwu as an Oracular Deity. For over three hundred years, this cult exploited the Igbo world by instigating inter-village wars that destroyed the economy and political stability of the place. Captives from those wars were sold as slaves through Aro traders who operated the oracle. The oracle was also used for adjudication in land disputes. It is probable that the operators of this oracle initially occupied a grove in Awo-Omama in the more central Igbo area, before later migrated to a more secluded and obscure place in Arochukwu where they changed the name of the deity and its mode of operation. All villages in Arochukwu were not involved in the operation or even understood the secrets of Ibin Ukpabi as the Aro Oracular Deity.

The close relationship with Chukwu during man's age of innocence and purity underscores the views of the fall held around Abakiliki and Ikwo in Northeast Igbo Subculture area and Ukwa, Azumini, Ndoki and Obehie, in the South-south Igbo Subculture Area. In these places the symbolism of mortar and pestle which the woman used in pounding her food, is interpreted in a subtle way to imply man's descent to carnality and sexual knowledge contrary to God's instructions. Man's reprobate state constituted a sort of profanation of the purity and sanctity of God who could not tolerate impurity. In order to avoid further profanation of his purity and holiness, God withdrew a little further away from man. There is no other part of Igbo territory that tries to explain the distance between God and man as a result of sexual misdemeanour on the part of man.

The argument whether God is **Deus Otiosus** or **Deus Remotus** in African Traditional Religion *is an over flogged issue.* It is superfluous to be repeated here. Nonetheless, the Igbo still see God as an immanent deity who can be appealed to in the greatest hour of need. From pithy sayings, names, proverbs, structure of society, ejaculatory prayers and wishes, one observes that the Igbo do not see God as a remote or absentee deity.

3.3   The Sun and Moon move up to live in the Sky
(From Ikwo North-east Igbo Sub-culture Area)

Many years ago, the sun (*Anyanwu*) and the Sea were good friends. That time the sun lived close to the earth and gave light and warmth to the people. There was no night at all because the sun was very close to people's homes. The sun often paid visits to the compound of **Imo Nwe Mmiri (the sea god that owns the ocean).** The sea had a very large compound and spread to a very large expanse of land. There are other parts of the land space that Imo did not occupy. One day, Anyanwu, though large and flamboyant in his own way, wondered why his friend Imo Nwe Miri does not visit him at all. The sea does not return the sun's several visits. One day, the Sun went to his friend's house (Mmiri) and asked him, 'why is that you and your relatives do not like to visit me as often as I do? I come to your house regularly and at times bring my sons and daughters (Kpakpando i.e. stars) to your house?'

Water (Mmiri) apologised for his inability to return any of the visits. He explained to his friend- Anyanwu- that his problem was that of space. 'You see, my friend,' said Water to the Sun, 'your compound is too small to accommodate me and my family when we visit you.' My entourage is a large one. You know I have a large family and many of the members of my family would like to accompany me when I come. I am afraid, we might drive you and your family away, when we arrive… if you really want me to visit you, continued Water, 'you must enlarge your compound. I must warn you that my people are very used to large space and they may damage your property if they are not adequately accommodated when they arrive' Their friendship was not meant to bring distress to any of the parties involved.

The Sun promised to build a larger compound as a part of his preparation to welcome his friend who was to visit him with his family. He embarked on extension project and his wife- *Onwa-* (the Moon) made a lot of contributions to the new expansion work. Soon afterwards, the project was completed and another invitation was sent to Water. A date was fixed and both parties prepared for it.

Imo Nwe-Mmmiri got his entire household together and set out to visit his friend Anyanwu in his home. He took with him a large retinue including all the fish, crocodiles, sea dogs, animals, whale, frog, crab, sea weeds, big plants and many other aquatic animals and plants. On arrival, Water stood outside and asked if the space was large enough to let him and his entourage in. The Sun shouted in excitement that there was enough space for everyone. The Water entered and gradually began to spread to all the rooms, flooding everywhere, tides rising, fish swimming, plants spreading their leaves, frogs and toads, croaking. There was confusion as the Water's large entourage struggled for space. The guests covered the Sun and his own family and yet there was not enough space for some other members of the Water Family to get in. Soon the Water covered everywhere and the host was driven out of his home. The Sun and Moon with the Stars were compelled to leave immediately upwards to create more space for their guests. In Igbo Traditional society, it is unfair for the host to keep his guests standing. That is why the Sun and Moon moved to live *'upstairs'* and allowed his guests to occupy their ground floor accommodation. Today, the Sun lives on the Sky while the Water occupies the land space and yet looking out for more spaces to occupy.

COMMENTS

The Igbo idea of the Planets is still not clearly articulated. It is still believed that the Sun is not as big as the Sea that is found everywhere on earth surface. The Sun is only in one place but Sea occupies different parts of the Earth. This presupposes the age of the earth surface- once covered by water but later receded

    i.   The myth underscores Igbo warning that one should cut one's coat according to one's cloth. One should try not to associate with someone too big for his position. Friendship should be with one' own social equals. The idea of deluge at certain period of Igbo history is hereby endorsed.

    ii.   The ecological confusion and natural disaster humans experience up to now can be traced to the problems caused by inter-personal relationship in the spiritual realm The physical destruction has its root and cause in the confusion and crisis in the realm of the spirit.

iii. Previously, there was quiet and order in the ecosystem until the rhythm and order in the universe became disorganised by unwholesome personal intercourse. It is in an attempt to create some relationships that humans disrupt the order in the universe. The unwholesome friendship and exchange of visit brought about dislocation in the universe.

CHAPTER FOUR
THE PRESENCE OF DEATH IN THE WORLD

4.1   Death is introduced by a slow Messenger
(Version from Isiala-Ngwa, South Igbo Sub Culture Area)

Chukwu wanted to destroy the world because of many evils in it. The information was leaked to man on earth. There was fear all over the place. The council of elders met immediately to discuss how to face the challenge. Two groups held opposing views. The first group did not want Chukwu to introduce death at all because it would deprive humans the opportunity to enjoy eternal life here on earth. Besides, it would deplete the population of human race on earth. The other group did not completely reject the idea of introducing death. They suggested that it would be introduced in such a way that all human beings would not die at the same time. It should come in piecemeal. Chukwu was present at one of the meetings and listened to both sides of the argument. The elders could not arrive at a consensus. This was the time Chukwu lived with man and woman on earth before he left them for Heavens above. He did not interrupt the discussions but listened with rapt attention. He did not act immediately but gave humans time to reconcile their views and agree on a point. While the impasse was on, Chukwu left for heavens and departed from his home on earth where he lived close to man.

Chukwu later reminded humans of his plans to introduce death. He informed them that the population of the earth was increasing at a very fast rate and needed to be controlled. The elders met again but could not reach consensus in their second meeting. Each group decided to send words across to Chukwu independent of the other. Chukwu should then decide on what he wanted to do after hearing from both sides.

The group that did not want death at all decided to send the dog, a very friendly animal to man and a very fast runner to take the message to *Chukwu*. They felt that the dog would carry the message fast enough. Chukwu would equally act fast on getting their views that he should not introduce death. The other group, on the other hand, decided to send a very wise animal that would be able to convince Chukwu to introduce death in a very careful way. They considered the Tortoise- *(Mbekwu)* the wise animal to do the errand although he was a slow moving animal. The two groups agreed on a day to send the two emissaries to Chukwu with different messages. The journey would be a long one. It would involve crossing seas, deserts, climbing mountains, going through forests, and bushes. Both animals set out early in the morning for the long trip. The agreement was that the one who got *to Chukwu's* house first and delivered his message would be the decision that would be accepted by the whole community.

The dog ran fast amidst the cheers and admiration the first group that sent him. At midday, he felt hungry and entered a small bush along the way and had a good lunch, which made him fall fast asleep immediately. The tortoise, on the other hand, went on slowly but steadily until it passed the dog who was still asleep after the heavy lunch. The tortoise eventually got to Chukwu's house first. He gave the decision of his group to Chukwu who accepted man's choice of Chukwu to introduce death. Chukwu accepted the method as a means of controlling population explosion on earth. Chukwu thanked the tortoise and sent him on his way home to give his approval to man on earth. The dog who was fast asleep got up and ran straight to Chukwu's abode and got there after the tortoise had left. Chukwu told him that he had already taken a decision on the recommendations the first group sent to him. He will introduce death on regular basis and not a one-off event. The dog felt disappointed. He took the sad news home.

The tortoise got home early enough and announced that Chukwu had agreed to introduce death as demanded by humans. Those who were really against this view were angry that Chukwu accepted the Minority Opinion. Later the dog arrived to tell humans that Chukwu had approved the suggestions which the tortoise brought before he arrived. Thenceforth, Chukwu began to send death to kill humans on earth. Man's life on earth became short. No one will live eternally on earth again.

COMMENTS

Death is man's chief enemy and he tries to avoid it by all means. The roles played by the two messengers emphasise the need to be careful in any competition. No opponent should be taken for granted. It is important not to under-rate the ability of any competitor. Besides, the myth underlines a few Igbo philosophies in life:

      i.   Dedication to duty- one on duty must concentrate on the job and not to allow any distraction.

     ii.   Pride goes before a fall- the fast moving dog felt proud and ignored some unforeseen circumstance

   iii.   Wisdom is a cardinal Igbo virtue. A wise man will win a foolish strong man.

   iv.   The Igbo believe in the maxim that 'slow and steady wins the race'- those who are always in a haste are usually in a waste

    v.   For God, the first decision and statement stands and any other later version is not acceptable.

   vi.   The myth underlines the Igbo view that humans contribute to the idea of death- it is not arbitrary decision of Chukwu to introduce it. Man's choice is involved- the Igbo is no Fatalist! Choice is open to him.

The Igbo still believe that man is partly responsible for his plight on earth. They are no fatalists. Death may not be avoided but untimely death is avoidable.

4.2   No Distinction in Death
(Version from Avu, Owerri, South Igbo Subculture Area. Similar version from Eha-Alumona, Ikem and Obollo-Eke and Obollo –Afo, North Igbo Subculture Areas)

Man was very sad when he discovered that Chukwu endorsed the Minority Report brought back by the Tortoise by allowing death on earth. The introduction of death frightened man. God sent Mr Death to get at the first victim. He went straight to young people to kill them. They were upset and surprised that Death came to them. They pleaded with him to give them some more time to enjoy life on earth. They argued that they were young and had not spent time on earth to enjoy its beauty and bounty. It was wrong for death to kill them in their prime. So they referred Mr Death to the old people. Their argument was based on justice.

Death moved fast to the old people and wanted to strike them. They in turn, asked death to leave them alone. They pleaded that they had suffered a long time, bringing up their children, tilling the ground, building houses, and had not had time to enjoy all that they had laboured for. They thought that they would begin to enjoy life in its abundance in old age as a reward for hard work. They therefore asked Death to go to the little children who had not made any useful contribution to the development of the earth. Death listened to their reasonable argument and left them. This was based on sound logic

From there, Death went to strike the children who were playing at the town square. They cried and pleaded with Death that they were young, innocent and had not contributed to the corruption in the world.

It was the adult who had polluted the world with sin, hatred, sexual immorality, stealing and cheating. They said they were not mature enough to follow death. They rather asked death to go to the infants who were unable to do anything yet and whose presence in the world had not been 'regularised or recognised' through initiation rites and ceremonies. They were substantially not humans yet until they were initiated into some big secret societies and undergone some rites of passage in society. The infants, on their part, pleaded to be left alone

This was a serious and clean moral argument since precious and harmless ones had done nothing to deserve premature departure from the universe. They had just entered the world and justice demands that they should be given more time to prove their mettle. Death was again convinced by their logic. He therefore decided to go to the poor. On getting there, the poor wept. They told him that they had suffered all their life. They had been abused, hurt, cheated and exploited by the rich and other more privileged people who stole their land, took their wives, enslaved them and denied them the basic amenities of life. They pleaded with Death to leave them alone but rather go to the rich who had enjoyed much of the bounty of the earth. This was a very solid argument based on mercy.

When Death got to the rich, he thought they would be ready to follow him. The rich rather tried to convince him to leave them alone. They presented Death with a long list of programmes uncompleted-building plans, purchase of land in many places, many acres of land to farm, many wives and children to look after, many cows and sheep that would suffer if they leave them uncared for. Many people who depended on the rich people would starve. The rich also requested Death to allow them long time to organise their assets and wealth before leaving the earth.

A few shrewd rich people asked Death secretly if he would accept some money from them and leave them alone to live here on earth forever, contrary to Chukwu's arrangement and instruction. They offered to give Death some money so that he would leave them and their relatives to live here on earth forever. Death at this point got confused because each argument was logical enough. He decided to go back to Chukwu to ask for clarification and renewal of his mandate. He went back empty handed and explained everything to Chukwu. Here the rich could have used bribery to escape death.

Chukwu got annoyed with Death and blamed him for being stupid to listen to arguments, which humans presented. It was a matter that needed urgent finality in which there should be no further discussion. As a punishment for his failed mission, Chukwu struck Death with blindness and deafness. Death became blind and deaf- could not see anyone's face or hear any one' reasons however logical or true. God sent him again to the world with a heavy iron rod to hit however he meets irrespective of age, gender, status, character, etc. That is why Death makes no distinction today in his mission to kill. He hits black, white, rich, poor, young, old, tall, short, religious, non-religious, man, woman, ugly, beautiful, etc. Death is blind and deaf and therefore can hit any time, anywhere, any person. He does not accept any pleadings. He strikes with a touch of absolute finality and heeds no appeal.

COMMENTS

Death is universal and often has no regards for anybody's position and status. The Igbo believe that if any group had succeeded to convince death against the other, only a few people would be dying. No group can escape death and no one directs death to any one to kill. No one directs nor commands death. A few Igbo names and proverbs emphasise Igbo philosophical hatred, fear and concepts of death. Such personal names include:

Onwueme-enyi: Death has no friends; Death does not befriend anyone.

Onwubuariri- Death brings misfortune and dishonour- death is the cause of misfortune and let down.

Onwuzuligbo- Death is all over Igboland, - it is universal

Onwuchekwa- Death should hold on

Onwubiko- Death, please spare me

Onwuamaegbu- Death kills wrongly- i.e. he does not kill the very people who should die especially bad people

Onwuatuegwu- Death does not fear to kill, or Death does not frighten me

Onwueyiagba- Death does not give an appointment- he comes any time

Onwudinjo- Death is evil and wicked

Onwuzulike- Death should go and rest

Onwuamaeze- Death does not respect the King or does not know the King

Onwura- Death should leave me

Onwuka- Death is stronger than people

Onwuegbuna- Death should not kill

Akuegbo-onwu- Wealth does not prevent death

Egwuatuonwu- Death does not fear at all- so he can strike even the most respected person.

Human beings have feared death for a long time. Man has tried to face the stark reality of death and its devastating blow by adopting several strategies. These include good moral character, sacrificial rites, procreation of many offspring, polygamy, wearing of charms to protect life, etc.

CHAPTER FIVE
MAN, DEITY AND NATURAL ECOLOGY

5.1 Mbaa River leaves Mbara –Owerre for Ugiri
(From Ezihe Mbano, Isu-Ama sub-unit of the South Igbo Subculture Area)

Mbaa River whose present source is at Isi-Nkwo Mbaa Ugiri- Ama in Isiala Mbano Local Government Area of Imo State, used to occupy an expanse of land called Mbara Owerre in the distant past. The place is located between Ezihe in the North and Amaraku in the South, Umuezefeke Ugiri in the west and Agbaja in the east. These towns share the various parts of the expanse of land, which is called Mbara Owerre. The large area of land is still there with a huge valley that shows some river capture or a dry old riverbed in the distant past.

No one knew when the Mbaa Deity moved into Mbara Owerre in the distant past. The deity moved into the area in the night and came with his river and occupied an empty space of land. This frightened the men and women of the area when they got up in the morning and found the whole land mass covered by water. The Deity lived there with his River for several years. He provided the people with water to cook, wash, drink, fish. A lot of farming developed by the side of the River and men and women developed a strong agricultural base near the riverbanks. The Deity moved with a priest who lived at a very small hut by the Mbaa River banks and maintained the shrine there. People were happy to have a big river close to them and it provided them a lot of opportunities. The priest lived quietly and offered rituals to the river god. None of the elders came to him to show hospitality or thank him and the deity for coming to live in their home. In spite of the numerous benefits people got from the presence of the Deity and its river, no one came to ask the priest how they could show appreciation or hospitality to him. They did not molest the priest at all but rather took his presence for granted.

After several years, the Deity felt that the surrounding towns should have come to show appreciation to him by offering sacrifices of thanks for the numerous benefits they derived from his presence in their area. He decided to send his priest to the elders of the towns around to inform them that he needed a light-skinned man and light-skinned woman- **nwoke –ocha na nwanyi –ocha-** They did not understand what the offering meant. They were not involved in Slave Trade and Human Sacrifice. The demand was too bizarre for them. They consulted an oracle. The diviner explained to them that the deity wanted them to offer a man and a woman to him as pages that would serve at his shrine. This frightened the people. They met several times to discuss how they could obtain two living human beings for such ritual sacrifice. They thought the deity was really making a very hard demand from them. No one was willing to spare his son or daughter .It was difficult to obtain male or female slave either. No one was willing to offer himself as a cult slave. The deity sent them several reminders but the people were afraid and could not do anything.

While this was going on, some elders from Ugiri-Ama met together and decided on a pact. They felt that they could try with some substitutes. A very wise old man from there told his people to offer the deity a white cock and a white hen since it was difficult to obtain living human beings. The whole of the council nodded their approval and got a white cock and a white hen. A few days later, they presented the gifts to the priest of Mbaa Deity who offered them to the River god. Soon after that, the deity decided to move to the town that offered the sacrifice. So on one Nkwo Market day, Mbaa Deity moved out of Mbara Owere with its river and finally settled at its present location at Isi-Nkwo Mbaa. This move was done before dawn and no living human being knew when it took place. Those who went to Mbara Owere early morning to fetch water were disappointed, as they saw nothing but dry gully and empty valley. Since that day, Mbaa River has been at Isi-Nkwo Mbaa and Mbara Owere has reverted to its former dry empty expanse of land. The Mbaa River has up till today its source in Ugiri- Ama at Isi-Nkwo Mbaa.

5.2 Otammari River Leaves Avu for Ihiagwa and Nekede (Version from Avu, South Igbo Subculture Area)

The Earth Goddess has many sons. Otammiri is one of them. When he grew up into manhood, he told his mother that he had decided to live at Avu. He found that there was a large uninhabited expanse of land in that area. Otammiri settled at the portion of land in front of the shrine of Umuodo, which is the chief deity of Avu town. The Umuodo deity who is female might perhaps have attracted Otammiri to come to settle at Avu. Otammiri took his river along with him when he moved into Avu.

After a long time, Otammiri demanded two human beings (a man and a woman) - from Avu community. The two people who would be offered to the deity as his cult slaves would live permanently at the shrine and run errands for Otammiri. The demand for human cult slaves was a real difficult thing for the community. No one was ready to offer his or her relatives for such services. Besides, it was difficult that time for the community to obtain a slave from any one. The town elders met several times to deliberate on how to meet the demands of the deity. Unfortunately they felt that they could not meet with the demands of Otammiri deity. The deity waited for a long time for the community to respond positively to its demands.

When the deity discovered that the Avu community was unable to meet up with his demands of offering him human beings,- a man and a woman- he decided to move out of the town in a quiet way. People were still in bed when they woke to see that the stream had gone to Ihiagwa. The departure left Avu dry. No sooner the deity settled at Ihiagwa and Nekede, than he made similar demands of two human beings from the community. The elders again consulted a diviner who advised them to make an offering with two lizards- one female and another male- to the deity. Soon after that, the Otammiri deity decided to settle permanently in Ihiagwa and Nekede and allowed its river to run through the towns. That was why Otammiri River runs through the towns of Ihiagwa and Nekede while Avu became dry up till today. The River Otammiri does not flow through Avu.

Otammiri later sent a message to Ogu, the oldest man in Ihiagwa, after a long time. The message was meant for Ihiagwa and Nekede people. Ogu was asked to tell the two towns of Ihiagwa and Nekede 'catch an Ovu (Obu)' – an owl- and meet Otammiri for an important discussion the next morning. Nekede got up early in the morning and began a long search for an Ovu throughout the neighbouring bushes. He spent a long time in the bush but caught no Ovu. Ogu who got the message, as an old man, understood the implications and asked Ihiagwa to meet Otammiri early in the morning. Before dawn, Ihiagwa was at Otammiri's gate while Nekede was still in the bush hunting for Ovu. Otammiri waited a long time for Nekede to arrive. When he could no longer wait, he decided to make Ihiagwa who was there already, the Regulator of the Traditional Calendar of the communities around. Thus Ihiagwa became the first town in Igboland to be given the power and right to act as the Custodian of Igbo calendar of festivals. At every meeting of the people, Ihiagwa would be the first to arrive. Ihiagwa would fix the dates for all Igbo annual festivals, time to clear the bush, plant the crops, harvest and eat new yams. Nekede and other neighbouring communities had to depend on Ihiagwa to inform them of the seasons and dates for all annual festivals. Thus Otammiri established the leadership of Ihiagwa over other neighbouring towns. Other towns would wait till Ihiagwa had celebrated its festivals before they fix theirs.

Ihiagwa people have maintained that leadership role of being the first to do anything since then. Ihiagwa sets the pace, leads, blazes the trail and others follow.

5.3 Adazi Gets Water
(Version from Awka, Northeast Subculture Area)

Chukwu sent down an old man from the sky to the town of *Adazi Nnukwu*. The bearded old man who was sent down had nowhere to build his house because the whole land space had been occupied. He went to another man in the town to ask for a portion of land to build his house. Adazi was known for being very kind and friendly to people and especially visitors and strangers. The visitor from Chukwu pulled his long grey beards and the whole area was covered with water. This frightened the people living in the area but they did not harm the man but refused to offer him a piece of land he demanded. The man then moved to Umuowelle in Agulu and requested for a piece of land to build a house. He asked for a part of the large forest that existed at the outskirts of the town. The Umuowelle people replied that the entire forest did not belong to them alone. A part belonged to Nri. Later Umuowelle and Nri met together and decided to offer the forest to the visitor.

Soon after that, the man set up a house there. On touching his long beards again, the whole forest became filled with water. Trees and leaves in the forest were covered by water. The water spread fast and covered a large area. This situation terrified the people who consulted an oracle to ascertain what to do to remedy the situation. The oracle told them to keep back the water by throwing out broken pots and wood into it. The entire community came out and brought out broken pots, pieces of wood and threw them into the rising water. Surprisingly the water level receded and collected into a small gully. That pocket of water that collected in the gully formed what we know today as Agulu Lake.

The people of Adazi Nnukwu performed some ritual sacrifices and part of the lake moved back to Adazi town. That part of the water divided into three and became the big streams that flow through the town till today. Adazi performed another ritual and the streams increased. They allowed the three to spread to Oraukwu, Uke and Obosi. The people of Adazi Nnukwu were kind enough to allow the other towns to benefit from the presence of the streams. Till today, Adazi is known as a very generous and kind town. This traditional kind nature of the town also made it welcome the Christian missionaries in the early 19th Century and this led to the building of big churches and hospital in the town. Adazi is one of the strongest centres of Christian religious faith in Igboland.

5.4   Imo River decides to live in Umuopara, Umuahia (From Umuopara Umuahia, South Igbo Area)

The first man sent down by Chukwu to live in Umuopara had no water to drink. The town was dry. He lived alone and had no neighbours from whom he could get water or fire. The man's name was Opara- meaning First Son. He was believed to be the first son of Chukwu- the Supreme Being. Each time he needed water, Opara would go to a very distant town for it. He suffered a lot in some of his long trips to get water from distant towns. He depended on the rains, which fell once every four years. He bought big pots and filled them with rainwater whenever it rained in those days.

Opara met ***Chukwu Nwe Imo*** (the Supreme God who owns Imo River) in one of his numerous long treks in search of drinking water. Opara pleaded with this deity to come and settle in his town. The deity saw Opara as a very kind and friendly person. He fell in love with Opara and showed him some sympathy when he heard of the difficulties he encountered in getting drinking water. So Chukwu Nwe-Imo agreed to come to live in Opara's town on the condition that:

i. He Chukwu-Nwe- Imo would only pass through Opara's house but would not end there.

ii. Opara and his people would worship the deity and offer him sacrifice

iii. No woman would come to the river to fetch water or bathe during her period of menstruation

iv. The male and female snakes, which live in the river, should not be killed because they are sons and daughters of the deity.

v. No one should be stopped from fetching water from the river that passes through Opara's house

vi. The water is the personal property of Chukwu and not that of Opara and his children.

Opara accepted the conditions and went home. The deity moved out one night and passed through Opara's home. When Opara got up early one morning, he saw the Imo River pass through his house and felt happy. He called his children and offered sacrifices to Chukwu. The children had never seen water of that magnitude before. They were afraid to jump into it to swim or collect water. Later, they began to play by the riverbanks and enjoyed the presence of Imo River in their place. Opara and his family called their neighbours to come and draw water from the river that passed through their house. Every year, Opara and his family offered sacrifices to the deity in appreciation of his benevolence. Chukwu asked him to call the name of the water Imo – meaning Overflowing greatness. Since that time, the river has been known as Imo

River and it flows through many towns. Everyone is allowed to come to the river to fetch water or bathe and swim. Opara's children became *UMUOPARA- Children of Opara.*

COMMENTS: 5.1-5.4

The myths of man, deity and the natural ecology point to man's responsibility and God's overruling power and authority in the universe. The Igbo worldview does not present man as a helpless pawn in the hands of an overpowering and angry deity. Man is often responsible for the success or failure he encounters in his life endeavour. Fatalism is to a great extent ruled out from the Igbo perception of the Universe. Man's failure on his own part may lead to long term socio economic problems while his one day's success might equally bring an overwhelming blessing to many generations yet unborn.

Furthermore, there is an implicit evidence that the Igbo life is a communal one. No one is an island to himself. It is society where one man's success may bring joy and blessings to the entire community and the neighbourhood. His careless or deliberate misdemeanour may bring calamity to the whole people around. The more he shares his blessings, the more they increase. There is joy and blessing in sharing gifts and it is believed that the deities enjoy the praise when humans relate peacefully with one another.

In the case of Avu, we notice again the error of literalism. The Igbo speak in an oblique mythical terms that at times confuse outsiders and the uninitiated. Note the problems of ingratitude on the part of humans. Even the deities appreciate expressions of gratitude. The departure of the Mbaa Deity from the Mbara Owerre is a clear evidence of two fatal errors- literal understanding and lack of gratitude. These should be checked in Igbo relationships.

5.5 Enmity Between Ogbuide River and Urashi River
(From Awo- Omama, South Igbo Subculture Area)

Ogbuide and Urashi Rivers are tributaries of Njaba River. They are usually called Ada Njaba- meaning *Daughters of Njaba*. This means that they are close tributaries that branched off from the main River Njaba and flowed to two different towns. Every village where the tributary of River Njaba passes through gives it a specific name that distinguishes it from what it is called in any other place. Yet it is the same river following from the same source. For instance, in Awo-Omama, particularly at a place called **Ukwu-oji,** the tributary of River Njaba is called *Ugha Mmiri-* meaning *—showers of water and rain*

Ogbuide and Urashi were close friends in the past. They were so intimate that they did many things together. In one of their discussions, they agreed to kill their bad children that had been bringing bad names to them. It was discovered that the sons of these two people had been notorious and each time bringing disgrace to the two deities- Ogbuide and Urashi. They set out days for the execution of the first notorious son and both agreed that Urashi would bring his first. On the agreed date, Urashi brought out his son and the two deities swallowed him up.

The following day, Ogbuide was to bring out one of his sons. Unfortunately, he failed to keep to the terms of agreement reached with his friend whose own son they had eaten the previous day. Urashi felt disappointed and let down by a trusted friend. From that day, he resolved not to have anything to do with Ogbuide whom he began to regard as a cheat and great fraud. Thus a great misunderstanding and hatred developed between the two former close friends. As the enmity and bad spirit grew, a barricade was built between them. This created a very conspicuous demarcation between them. Their boundaries became clearly marked. This demarcation stopped the children of one from crossing over to play with the children of the other. Since that day, no one could collect water from one river and pours it into the other. If that happens, the water flows black to the source. In other words, since that demarcation was built, if water from Ogbuide River flows into Urashi, it is returned back immediately. If any one collects water and pours it into any of the rivers, that same quantity of water will flow back to its source. That was the end of any close contact and relationship between the two. No fish from one river swims to the other and no drop of water from one flows into the other. It is indeed a very great enmity till today. It is impossible to put water from the two rivers into one pot. The container breaks and the water flows out. No animal, frogs, fish, or plants from one river survives in the other.

COMMENTS

The two rivers are close to each other but hitherto there is no real contact whatsoever. It is difficult to believe that a mystical division exists and one can easily recognise that the water from the two rivers can hardly remain in one container. The myth tries to underline the Igbo disapproval of dishonesty, breach of contract, fraudulent deal, and insincerity. Honesty and integrity should guide any interpersonal relationships in any society. They Igbo emphasise this ethical norms in any relationships.

5.6   Ami-agba Leaves Ogwugwu Valley
(From Oraukwu, Northwest Igbo Subculture Area)

One of the biggest streams in the ancient world was Ami-Agba, which was in Oraukwu town in Idemili Local Government Area of Anambra State. It was one of the sources of water supply to the inhabitants of the world in those days. Many people from different parts of the world came to Ami-Agba to fetch water for domestic use. It was unfortunate that many people who lived around the stream used to throw in a lot of dirty things into the stream. This annoyed the deity who sent notes of warnings to the people through the priest of Ogwugwu Deity. This warning came to the people several times but they did not heed it. Some girls from the village went to Ami- Agba stream to wash their clothes on one sunny afternoon. A sudden sound was heard and thunderous noise filled the air. The girls got highly terrified and threw away their clothes they were about to wash in the stream. They fell down and could not easily get up because of the trauma of the frightening experience. When they eventually regained consciousness, they looked up and could not find the stream again. It was a big surprise and even a shock to them that the body of water they saw a few minutes earlier, had completely disappeared. They saw a large expanse of dry land. The girls raised an alarm that attracted large number of people from the neighbouring villages including those from Ubenabo who came when they heard the distress call of the girls. The people were greatly terrified. Many began to offer sacrifices to the deity in order to regain its favour and goodwill. The deity did not pay attention to their offerings. A large gully emerged immediately near the *Oye Olisa* market in Oraukwu. There is still a very big gully in Oraukwu.

COMMENTS

The withdrawal of Chukwu to the Heavens above or the loss of opportunity by man is usually attributed to human inability to understand or obey the divine. Man's misfortune is in most cases the result of Man's disobedience. In Igbo traditional religion, forgiveness is not usually emphasised even after one has repented and confessed. It was a type of Casuistic and Apodictic Legal Systems

5.7 Atta Orlu Lost Opportunity to have Water in her town. (Version from Orlu, Isu-ama Subunit of South Igbo Area)

Atta is in Orlu Senatorial Zone of Imo State. It is a very big town, which has no water at all. There are many wells in the community. The villagers travel far every day to look for water. Chukwu was very friendly with the founding father of Atta town. He asked him as his friend to meet him one early morning. The man left his house in time to meet his friend Chukwu as scheduled. On getting there, Chukwu asked him what he would like to eat- dry fish (ready cooked food) or raw food implying going out to till the ground and grow his own food and harvest it and cook it before eating. The man preferred the ready-made food, thereby refusing to go out to till the ground.

By deciding to accept ready cooked food from Chukwu, the man invariably chose not to till the soil, fish in any water, experience rainfall or soil his hands by tilling the ground during the wet season. Chukwu was disappointed that his friend made such a careless choice of easy going life. From that day, Atta did not get water ponds, streams or rivers in the town. This led to severe heat and drought that prevented the people from farm work. Men have to travel long distances to look for drinking water. Chukwu withheld rain and this worsened the already bad situation. Since that time, Atta has no natural source of drinking water- no streams, no rivers and no springs. The people struggled to dig deep into the soil to look for water. That was the beginning of wells that one finds in different parts of the town which people sunk in their compounds and in town squares and open places. As time went on, many young people turned to trading instead of farming. Men and women learned to ride bicycles and even young children began riding bicycles and used them to travel to neighbouring towns to fetch water from Njaba and Ogbuide Rivers.

COMMENTS

The seriousness of the dry nature of Atta town has made her people resort to trading as a means of livelihood. This has in effect produced many rich traders and business people in the town. Atta is today seen as one of the richest Igbo towns where young men and women have created wealth through long distance trading. Today many rich people in Atta have built up their beautiful homes with boreholes sunk everywhere for people to come and draw water.

The decision to go for the dry fish was man's explanation for most of the conditions in the world, which the Igbo see as partly due to man's choice and misbehaviour. The Igbo believe that it is better to go for hard work than accept the easy way of making a fortune. So many people prefer to struggle for their success than accept ready-made food or easy way to success. The Igbo proverb goes thus- give a child a piece of yam and you give him food for one day but give him a hoe and machete, you give him food for life. A similar proverb states that when you give a child fish, you have given him food for one day but give him hook and net, you provide him with food forever. Although Atta made a wrong choice at first, he did not succumb to begging or living a helpless life. He went out to struggle for success, hence his children have turned to become rich through trading. The Igbo still believe that a mistake can be corrected if the individual concerned realises his error and works hard to remedy the situation. As long as life remains, one can still achieve one's destiny.

CHAPTER SIX
MAN, MUSIC AND WARFARE

6.1   Origin of Dancing and Music
(Version from Asaba, Niger Igbo Subculture Area)

In the past, only a few men and women lived on the earth. Thick forests, seas and trees covered other parts of the universe. The big trees became the abode of many spirits, fairies, and gods. Some gods, occupied trees, rivers and streams. Some big trees were feared and respected as the abode of the gods. Besides, because of frequent harassment by human beings, the spirits and gods decided to live in the forests where they enjoyed a lot of quiet and uninterrupted peace. Most men and women would always bring minor or major problems to the gods by visiting the shrines of the gods and local spirits in the forests. This constituted a sort of nuisance to the spirits and gods.

The animals, on the other hand, decided to live in the forests to escape man's constant attack on them. Men go out daily to hunt animals for food. This has put many animals at risk of extinction. So many of their species have decided to live far inside the bush to escape the attack from man. It is only the cow, dog, sheep and fowls that live in the home with humans. Other animals that live in the bush feel threatened. Although humans eat the domestic animals, which also serve as pets, they do not kill them at the rate they hunt the wild animals.

A man went out to hunt games on one sunny afternoon. He chased an antelope, which ran very fast into a big bush **to** escape being killed. The man persisted in his chase and came to a part of the bush which looked like an open hall where the animals use as a rendezvous where they meet to relax when they are not looking for food or when they are not running away from hunters. The hunter did not find any human being there. There was no animal either. He suspected that the space was so beautiful that it must be a centre when people gather for games or refreshments. He hid himself behind some big trees to wait for the people who meet there to assemble. After awhile, the forest spirits began to assemble there for their usual evening party. Many birds, and animals began to arrive for the party. Many other spirits and gods also came along with their wives and children. They began to sing, clap, dance, and enjoy some jokes. Some of the birds sang beautifully while some of the animals played some musical instruments that produced melodious sounds. It was an evening of great joy and merriment for the animals, birds, spirits and the gods. Some of the big animals hummed the songs, while the gods shook their bodies and moved their legs in rhythmic and regular steps. Some of the young birds played flutes and whistle. The melody was really gorgeous. The hunter was thrilled as he watched the programme from his hiding place. He did not want any of the guests to notice that he was there. Many of the animals, and birds were so carried away in the party that they did not know that some one was hiding and spying them from somewhere.

The guests at the party dispersed at the end of the programme. Each went home. The hunter did not move immediately. He kept quiet till every one present had left. He finally left and on his way, began to imitate the spirits and the gods by humming some of the songs he heard. He moved his steps up and down, shook his body, hands, shook his head and smiled. Thus he began to practise what he saw the spirits and animals do in the forest. The hunter later got home that night and woke up his family that had already gone to bed. He taught the wife and children how to sing, dance and play some of the instruments. He improvised the drums and bands with pots, tables, stools, plates that he had in his house. Some of the domestic appliances were used as improvised instruments.

The members of the family enjoyed the late night entertainment the hunter brought home to them. So every evening, the family met, played some music, danced, smiled and entertained themselves. The words of the music did not matter so much to them. They concentrated on getting the rhythm right and the steps correspond with the rhythm. Some younger members of the family added some melody to the songs and the harmony was absolutely interesting.

COMMENTS

The Igbo believe that the forests are the abode of spirits and dangerous animals. Some people who died of some awful and dreaded diseases were thrown into the forests. Many dreaded the forests as hiding places for evil and dangerous spirits and gods.

i. Most Igbo medicine men, singers, diviners go to lonely places to meditate and relax. They do this primarily to escape from the noise of the surrounding environment in order to concentrate and perhaps listen to *the voice of the spirits and gods*. The seashore, quiet bush areas and desert places are places where some **men and women retire to for an inspired spiritual power. Initiation of novices into powerful cults takes place** in hidden forests and bushes.

The art of music is one that can be learnt through imitating an expert. Igbo music has a lot to do with religious spirituality. Many of the songs have powerful religious background.

6.2   The Origin of Owu Dance in Oguta
(Version from Oguta, Ogbahu, Atani, Odekpe, Ndoni,
Rivers and West Igbo Subculture Area)

The Owu Dance is an art that has to be learnt by both men and women. Although music is an art, it can also serve both aesthetic and economic values. It is now a profession that fetches men and women a lot of fortune in Igboland. Many people who are well trained in music can win favour and admiration from both leaders and people by merely putting up an excellent performance in the town.

Owu (Ogbu) Festival is one of the most important ceremonies in Oguta (Ugwuta). It is an ancient festival, which takes place in July every year. In the distant past, a man from Umutogwuma village saw a girl from Oguta who really won his admiration and love. He fell in love with her at first sight. He was so charmed by the girl's beauty that he struggled to marry her and eventually succeeded in marrying her. Unfortunately he had no money to pay for the traditional rituals and perform all the social ceremonies that were expected of a bridegroom. When the members of the girl's family asked for some gifts or money from the man as custom demanded, he complained that he had no money. He went to consult an Oracle to seek advice on what to do to retain the beautiful girl he had married. The diviner advised him that the deities would help him and have commanded him to entertain the parents of the girl and their families. In order to convince the parents-in-law of his love for their daughter and his seriousness to marry her, the man started to entertain them with a very beautiful music which the deities taught him on his way to his home after he had gone to visit the Oracle. The entire family was excited on watching the new brand of music they had never seen before. They were so excited and thrilled that they asked the man to teach them how to perform that sort of new music that no one in the community had ever seen. It was such a graceful and unique dance that the people decided to learn it. The bridegroom immediately got up and carefully taught them how to perform the new dance.

The King of the community heard about the new dance and asked the family to come to perform it in his palace. This attracted many people from different parts of the community. It was an excellent performance and every one present was thrilled. The king became very happy with the family and their new brand of music. He demanded the source and asked that members of the Royal Family be taught how to perform it. The Royal Dance Troupe came to the family to learn the styles of the new dance. The master dancer- the bridegroom came to teach the group sent by the King. From there, the King ordered that every member of the community must learn how to perform the new dance. Thence both adults and young people in the community learnt the dance. No member of the girl's family demanded money or gifts again from their son-in-law. The Owu became the town traditional ceremonial dance and any time the community gathered for their annual festival, the family must perform the Owu Dance or any group appointed to do so. The King's special Dance Group made weekly presentation at the King's palace to entertain him and his guests. That was how the town decided to make every prospective son-in-law present Owu Dance to his would-be parents in law. This became a part of the traditional marriage ceremony in Oguta. As years went by, Owu Dance became institutionalised as the Traditional Ceremony in Oguta and an integral part of the Marriage Rituals.

COMMENTS:

As already indicated, marriage in Igbo Traditional Society was not a money-oriented ritual ceremony. It has both social and religious dimensions in which the gods, ancestors and humans play prominent roles.

i.   It was social as well as religious. Both the families and the gods were interested in it.

ii.   traditional rulers in many parts of the Igbo society had professional entertainment groups that lived in the palaces.

iii. It is difficult to get into any Igbo festival that does not entail traditional dances.

iv.   Many artistic and gifted people were highly known and admired as modern celebrities today. Some dancers and skilful artists and carvers, singers etc were believed to have received their gifts from the goods.

6.3   Men and Warfare
(Version from Abiriba, Item, Ohafia, Ngwa, Ohanso, Ohanku, Ndoki, South Igbo Subculture Area)

Chukwu made women very powerful and strong in the beginning of the world. Many powerful women dominated their husbands and fought bravely when enemies attacked. Women were climbing palm trees, cutting down *iroko,* mahogany and ebony as well as **Ngwu trees**. Women had very serious disposition and acted as mothers and protectors of their families. Men would spend more time at the town square discussing politics and how to make money. But the women were the real controllers of the society.

One community attacked another village on a very cold night. They appealed to Chukwu for support. He sent women to go and fight the attacking enemies. Many of them left their little babies with their husbands and put on their loincloths and carried their guns. They matched like brave soldiers and went to do battle with the invaders.

The women demonstrated enormous power at the battlefield. Their gallant performance made their enemies retreat in shame.   The women belligerents burnt down the houses of their enemies, cut down their farms, looted their property and killed many domestic animals. In addition, they killed ten strong people there but on their part they had no casualties. They matched back home after this heavy battle.

They looked sad and quiet as they matched home. Each of them looked depressed and disappointed. Chukwu called them to his gate to welcome them and to enquire how the battle went. The powerful commander gave the war reports to Chukwu and expressed their disappointment that they could kill only ten people.

The next day, war broke out again between the town and another neighbouring community. This time it was over a small piece of land at the boundary. Chukwu collected another set of war implements- spears, guns, arrows, clubs, sticks, and gave them to the men this time. He asked the women to look after the homes while the men who had never gone to war before should this time experience what it takes to defend the town. The men went into battle and also distinguished themselves as strong people. Unfortunately for them, they did not kill any one except one weak disabled person who could not run out with others when the men attacked. They cut off the man's head and brought it home.

As the men were matching home, they began to sing songs of victory:

Odogwu! Odogwu   Enyi mba, Enyi   (DC)
Odogwu!   Enyi Mba Enyi

Nzogbu, Nzogbu, Enyi Mba Enyi
Nzogbu, Enyi Mba Enyi
Nzogbu

This song of victory depicts a very high sense of achievement and success. Chukwu was upstairs and looked out at a distance and saw many people coming home with songs and waving fresh palm fronds (Omu nkwu) showing that they are victorious. Chukwu sent one of his servants to meet the men at the gate to enquire of the results of the war and the cause of their jubilation and songs of excitement and exhilaration. The Commander of the men's army brought out the head of the disabled man they killed and presented it to Chukwu's servant in a big basket. He related how gallantly they fought and drove out the enemies. When Chukwu asked them the number of people they killed, the men proudly in a chorus tone thundered, **Only One Sir!** Chukwu was surprised and felt a little embarrassed. He there and then concluded that if women were allowed to continue to fight in wars, they would never be satisfied with any number of casualties. They would wipe out the entire human race. So Chukwu there and then commissioned men to be belligerents and stopped women from going into battlefield again. He warned the women not to touch or have any close relationship with their husbands while in battle field as that would distract the attention of men from concentrating on the main battle. From that day, men began to wear loincloth and carrying guns. Women were given kitchen knife and asked to be permanently confined to the kitchen and make sure that they cook good food for men and the children. Men began to use guns for other purposes- games and entertainments. At funerals, guns are fired to accord honour to men while none is fired for women. When a successful rich man takes title, his people greet him with 21- gun salute as a mark of great honour to him but that is not extended to Igbo women. Men became associated with gun. When a baby boy is born, people will present guns as symbol of greatness and power and as a mark that he would be a warrior to defend his people. Guns became personal property any young man must acquire on reaching adult age.

6.4   Women Excluded from participating in War (Version from Uburu, Okposi, North East Igbo Subculture Area)

In the distant past, both men and women went to war and fought side by side like great companions. Many powerful and brave women led the battle while some men were at the back carrying their bags. Some families were left unprotected and children had no one to look after them when husband and wife went to battle together especially where the woman was a fierce fighter. Later, Chukwu stopped women from going into the war fronts again. This was because of one ugly incident that took place in one of the battles. Men were asked in the past to keep off their wives before they entered the battlefield. Men wore serious charms on their hips before they went into battle. Many of them slept in trenches in the bush. Women on the other hand, did similar things and the powerful ones among them slept in the bush with men. Chukwu warned both men and women not to engage in any sexual act while in the battlefield. The medicine men and diviners who accompanied the belligerents to the battle field would ask both men and women to desist from engaging in any sexual act because that would neutralise the potency of the protective charms they wore to the battle. One woman dropped her gun at the middle of the night and smuggled herself to the part of the bush where her husband was laying ambush in the forest. Her husband was attracted to her and both had sexual relations in the trench. The next morning the enemy attached the troops and they were severely beaten. Many people died and the enemy drove them back over twenty miles. The town elders felt bad and went to the oracle to demand why they suffered such server defeat. They were told that a couple defiled the face the of the Mother Earth, the Earth Goddess, by having sex in the bush at night while the other combatants were lying ambush waiting to fight. The culprits were identified and the diviner asked the community to perform some purification rites. The people went back to the battlefield and achieved a resounding victory over their enemies and regained lost territory. From that day, the Earth Goddess, warned men not to take their wives to the battlefield again. Women began to stay at home with children and old people. No man was allowed to touch his wife or visit his family while in the battlefield. Newly married couple were allowed to stay away from the battle till after one year to enable the woman to get pregnant and stop worrying the husband when called up for national service in the army. The Earth Goddess ordered that no woman should be fired or shot in any battle. They were from that day regarded as *Non- belligerents* – including children. So no one should fire gunshots at women and children in any war in Igbo world.

COMMENTS

The two-versions point to the exclusion of women for different reasons. It is a pity women are used to explain any source of disappointment whenever Chukwu got angry at the society. The first version states clearly that women are naturally strong and powerful. Igbo women are brave and tough. They are known to be responsible holders of offices and efficient commanders whenever they are in positions of trust and power. Female soldiers and policewomen seem to be more powerful than their male counterparts. Men boast too much of what they can achieve but women are the real powers behind the success. One little achievement excites men. Women are not easily pleased with little achievement or success. The number of casualties they had over the enemies did not impress them. One alone made men come home with songs of victory-mark of arrogance and fulfilment. The empty vessels make much noise. Chukwu does not show partiality. The myth underscores the fact the Igbo believe that Chukwu would not like any part of human race to be wiped out by the other. God is the God of all Igbo people- i.e. Human Race according to Igbo worldview.

CHAPTER SEVEN
GOD AND OTHER DEITIES

7.1. Chukwu and the Mermaid
(From Alor, Northwest Igbo subculture Area)

The Mermaid (Eze-nwanyi bi na Mmiri), the Queen of the Oceans and Great Rivers, conspired with other deities to challenge the authority and supremacy of Chukwu- the Igbo Supreme God. She was known as a very beautiful deity and the patron deity of Beauty in the whole world. So this idea made her proud. The deities had a secret meeting and unanimously agreed to reject the authority of Chukwu. They elected one of them to be the leader when they dethrone Chukwu. They encouraged her to engage in contest with Chukwu to know who was more fashionable and popular. The contest would be over dressing habits. The Mermaid would challenge Chukwu to a contest to know which of them was more fashionable than the other. Chukwu laughed at the Mermaid when he heard of the secret meeting. He knew everything about the meeting and saw them when they were discussing the plans to dethrone him. He even heard all they discussed. This is because Chukwu is ubiquitous and is omnipresent and omniscient.

The deities sent a message to Chukwu that they would like to fix a contest between him and the mermaid. Chukwu accepted the challenge without argument. A day was fixed for it. Chukwu got ready before any other deity and sat on his throne in his palace. He sent one of his messengers – the Chameleon-(Ogwumagana) to fetch the mermaid to the village square where the contest would take place. The Mermaid emerged from the depth of the sea in gorgeous apparel that made her look cute and flashy. As she was coming out from the gate of her house, she saw the Chameleon on her doorsteps. She got angry immediately. She told her retinue of servants and ladies in waiting who were responsible for her wardrobe to take her back to her dressing room. She was angry to see the Chameleon wearing the same dress she was putting on for the contest. She felt that if the ordinary messenger who was sent to call her was dressed as gorgeously as she was, Chukwu would invariably dress in a more expensive robe than hers. She forgot to realise that the Chameleon's skin pigmentation would always correspond with the colours around him. She felt it was an insult to wear the same dress with a messenger of Chukwu who was getting ready to appear to challenge her. She went into her wardrobe to pick another expensive dress. This time it was a very expensive damask and velvet dress. She came out to the same place and found the Chameleon in the same dress she was putting on. She was putting on a set of royal regalia like bracelets, (**Kamenyi**), **Kalari**, na **ola-edo; ivory, jewelleries, elephant tusks, and gold trinkets**). The mermaid came out and saw the Chameleon putting on the same dress again as she was putting on. She thought that the chameleon went home to change to the new dress, which incidentally resembled hers. The third time, the Mermaid found the Chameleon came out again in the same dress with hers. She went in again to her chambers to put on a different dress only to come out to her gate to see the Chameleon in the same dress. She suspected that one of her neighbours might have been hiding somewhere to disclose to Chukwu the type of dress she wanted to put on. After several attempts to change to new dresses to the contest only to see Chameleon in the same dress she concluded that it was unreasonable to continue with the contest. She finally gave it up and concluded that if she were unable to beat the ordinary messenger of Chukwu, it would be impossible to beat Chukwu himself. She told her friends that

Ka funafuna di otua
Kedu ka funofuno ga-adi?

This means that if the messenger was so gorgeously dressed, how much more would Chukwu dress?

Chukwu later commended the Chameleon as a very smart messenger and rewarded him with gifts for doing a good job. He gave the Chameleon the unique ability to change his colour to match any environment as a way to protect itself from danger. The Igbo started to say of the Chameleon

O hu oji   O jiharia
O hu ocha, O chagharia

This means that if he sees a black pigmentation, he turns black but if red, it turns red too.

Since that time, no environment can outwit the chameleon. It must adapt its colour to match it. No one, - human or spirit- had since that day tried to challenge the power or wisdom of Chukwu. Initially, the gods felt that if the Mermaid defeated in the contest, in the area of beauty and fashion, another deity would stand and challenge Chukwu in the area of wisdom, strength or power. None has ever stood up to challenge Chukwu in any area of life.

COMMENTS

This myth explains the supremacy of Chukwu. No creature could compete with Chukwu in any contest. God is both wise and powerful. All creatures are believed to be his agents and as such could be used to carry out an errand for him to achieve a particular goal. All created beings are subject to Chukwu and the Igbo are not confused about Chukwu's supremacy. There is no confusion in Igbo pantheon.

i. the chameleon in some respects stand for a man who is capricious and should not be trusted. A person who changes his mind easily or renegades on any agreement is called a chameleon.

7.2   Chukwu stays in Ndi- Ezera
(From Ohafia, Cross River Igbo Subculture Area)

In the distant past, the Omukwu of Asaga Ohafia was staying at Ndi Awa Omukwu compound. People from different parts of the world consulted the Omukwu Deity at Asaga. The consultation could take place at any time of the day. The deity felt disturbed by the number of clients who came to him at any time of the day for consultation. He complained that he was being unduly disturbed because he was staying at **Ime-Ogo**- the ancestral part of the town where every one had easy access to him. Ndi Awa Omukwu, the shrine of the deity, was located in the central part of the town. The great deity needed a more secure and secluded place to stay to be saved from the unnecessary harassment by visitors.

The Deity spoke to one of the elders in Ohafia that he would like to move to Ndi- Ezera where he believed that people would not be coming too often at odd hours to disturb his private life. The elders met and decided to consult an oracle to confirm the request from Omukwu Deity. They decided to move the Obinkwa- the shrine to Ndi-Ezera that is a little away from the busy town centre. The Omukwu was a war hero ancestor who led his people to war and each time brought them victory. He wanted to move his shrine from the centre of the town to another part that was not easily accessible to every one but to those who really needed to see him. Omukwu did not want people to see him when he was coming from war. Moving from a little obscure place from the glare of the city, he could concentrate on some more important and serious needs than the frivolous things, which people brought to him.

COMMENTS

The myth of Omukwu is quite unique. It is the only known account where an ancestor had been made a deity. This may be a case of a mixture of history and myth. The Igbo ancestors are not placed in the same class of divine beings with the Earth goddess or patron deity like Idemmili. There is a famous temple called Omo- Ukwu Temple. The people built it in honour of this famous ancestor Uma Ukpai who founded Asaga. His descendants still live in Asaga till today. The temple is said to have been in existence for more than five hundred years. The Federal Government of Nigeria declared the Omu Ukwu temple a National Monument in 1964. The National Antiquities Commission has since then preserved this as one of the national monuments in the conutry.

7.3   Ishieke Goddess comes to Ugbene

An old woman arrived at Ugbene one evening. She arrived in a very mysterious circumstance. No one knew her name, her home, her background and in fact no one knew anything about her at all. Since no one knew her name, people called her **Ogoro** **Ugbene** – meaning the woman of Ugbene. She had the power to transform herself into a python- (**Eke**). The python is a totem animal in Ugbene.

A hunter accidentally killed this python on one hot afternoon. The head of the snake disappeared from the rest of the body. No one was able to explain how the head got severed from the body. The hunter's careless mistake by killing the python brought a lot of misfortune to the town. The people had no rain, no water and there was hunger everywhere. There was plague and many little children and old people suffered a lot and died. The elders met and decided to consult an oracle to ascertain the cause of constant epidemic and drought in the town. They were told to intensify the search for the missing head of the python.

They were told to cover it with a clean white linen cloth and give it a decent burial whenever they found it.

They carried out an intensive search for the missing head of the python. They got to a big hill where they found the upper jaw on top of the hill. This encouraged the distressed team of searchers who felt that their efforts had been rewarded by the supreme deity. They continued their search till they came to the foot of the hill and found the lower jaw. They picked it and fixed it to the upper part, which they had picked up at first. They took it home and buried it in a very secure place just as the diviner directed them.

The people discovered that two shrines sprang up from the two spots where the upper and lower jaws were picked up. The shrines became known as *Ishi-Eke*- meaning Head of Pythons. The spot where the upper jaw was picked up became known as *Ishieke Ugwu* because it was on top of a hill. The spot where they picked the lower jaw became *Ishieke Oda*- The two spots became sacred and automatically turned into centres of worship. Ishieke became the goddess in the town of Ugbene. Since then the *Egoligo Ugbene* festival is an annual ceremony in honour of the Ishieke deity. People believe that the goddess came in the form of the unknown old lady who visited the town on one evening.

7.4   Anyim Deity comes to Amaogwugwu (From South Igbo Subculture Area)

Amaogwugwu is a village in Ohuhu clan in Ikwuano Umuahia. A pretty middle aged woman arrived in the village called Umuhu in the heat of the day on one afternoon. She went straight to the people one after the other asking for a child to live with and at the same time for a piece of land to build a small hut. Her requests were turned down. In the first instance, no one in the entire village of Umuhu knew her. It was, therefore, unsafe to give her a child to live with. Besides, no one would like to give out a piece of land to an unknown visitor.

Land was a rare commodity in the community. There was high population density and therefore people did not find it easy to give out portions of land on lease to any person. Families owned most portions of land and no individual person has the right to give out any portion to any one, let alone to an unknown visitor. The two requests were difficult ones for the people of Umuhu. When the lady failed to get a piece of land to build her hut and a child to live with, she felt disappointed. She left Umuhu for another village- Amaogwugwu.

The lady made similar requests at Amaogwugwu. The community leaders and elders met and generously offered a place to the visitor to build a small hut. In place of a child, they offered her an egg which she gladly accepted. The egg was hatched and a chicken, which came out of it, became the ***child of Anyim***

The community discovered that the new visitor was no ordinary person. Her new hut was transformed overnight into a big shrine. The place became awe-inspiring and lovely. Flowers and beautiful shrubs began to grow by the side of the shrine. The new chicken turned out to be a son and grew up fast. In fear and admiration, the people began to worship the young lady and started going to her for help and prayers. People took their problems to her. She told them her name- Anyim. Her home became a very central place of pilgrimage and prayers. Different people from the town began to flock to the compound of Anyim. The barren women were told what to do to get children. The sick were given medicines for healing. The oppressed reported their cases to her. People of Amaogwugwu took all sorts of problems to Anyim. She was delighted to help any one who called on her for help. She became generous and benevolent to the people. She disappeared one afternoon just as she came and asked her son to continue to live there with the people. He worked there for a short time and disappeared also. He appointed a man to look after the shrine before he left. Since that time, the Anyim goddess has become the most popular deity in Amaogwugwu and people have continued to worship her as their patron deity. People from the neighbouring villages have been coming to seek help from the shrine of Anyim.

COMMENTS: 7.3 and 7.4.

The Igbo still perceive the origin of many deities in a rather vague incomprehensible manner. No one knows the origin of the deity (visitor) Some elders just told us that the deity came like a human being to dwell in the village. Epiphany of gods in the traditional society was a common phenomenon.

Men should be cautious, polite and hospitable to visitors. The Igbo insist on this ethical principle. You may not know when you entertain a deity or push him out. Igbo traditional laws insist on showing mercy and kindness to travellers or strangers. Children are advised not to taunt an unknown visitor especially if the visitor is disabled or appears like a beggar. Many vicious and wicked spirits can come incognito and many benevolent ones have come like that too.

CHAPTER EIGHT
KINGSHIP INSTITUTION AND
INHERITANCE IN IGBOLAND

8.1 Ibelenta Village excluded from Atani Kingship
(From Ogbahu, West Igbo Subculture Area)

In Ogbaru, (the present Ogbahu District which used to be under Onitsha Local Government of Anambra State,) the crown was made to rotate from one lineage to the other in order of seniority. There were six villages in Atani, which is a big town in Ogbahu. *Osebuluwa* (Supreme God) did not want any particular village or kindred to monopolise the privilege of supplying the candidate for the throne. On the 'death' of a ruling monarch a successor would be chosen from another village. That village will present a group of eligible candidates from among whom the community selects the best for the office. In Igbo traditional society, the *Igwe, Eze or Obi* does not die. He is regarded as a deity or representative personality. His death is euphemistically described as 'joining the ancestors'- a dignified way to lessen the pains of the trauma of the departure of a monarch. Among Ndi- Igbo, there is no hereditary monarchy. The council of elders elects every one.

The Ibelenta village supplied the king for some time. He was the Igwe Onowu who ruled in the distant past. He was a very powerful and despotic ruler. There was a very big tree beside his palace- *Owu Akpu* tree- (silk cotton tree). People suspected that witches used the tree as a rendezvous for their meetings especially at night. Some frightening birds like the owl would perch on the tree at night and produce such terrifying noise that the community would be in fear when they heard it. The king felt disturbed by the noise these birds produced especially at midnights. He ordered that the community should cut down that tree.

The Owu Akpu (silk cotton tree) in the area was regarded as a sacred tree. This particular one had existed for over two thousand years. No living person knew when it was planted by Osebuluwa – God. The king inspected the tree before it was felled. The people believed that the tree had mystical powers and associated it with a lot of healing and charms. They believed that the tree told the king not to allow its branches and trunk to fall on the ground on the day the people would cut it down. They should allow it to fall gracefully to the ground without breaking any of its branches. They should not treat a sacred object and personality with spite and levity. The tree was a symbol of power, respect and sacredness in Igbo society. It was a difficult task. The king did not know how to circumvent the problem of not letting the tree fall to the ground but must be carried and laid down gracefully and quietly with all the leaves and branches in tact. The King later accepted the condition which the big tree gave to him and decided to provide able bodied men in his community who would wait to receive the falling weight of the tree to avoid making it fall forcefully on the ground.

The King assembled the chiefs and community leaders to provide strong and able-bodied men in the community who would do the job. Every village nominated ten young and able-bodied men for this difficult task. No one dared question the authority of the king. Yet they knew how hazardous a task it was for the men to wait to hold a falling tree. The men raised their hands to collect the falling tree to hold it from falling directly on the ground. Unfortunately, the tree fell on them with a strong force and killed them. The incident annoyed everyone in the town. This was a town wide tragedy as every village lost ten able bodied men on the same day. The *Ojele Deity*, the patron deity of Atani got angry at the incident. The deity decided to punish the king- Igwe Onowu with blindness for causing the death of many young men in the town in one day. The priest of the deity warned the community not to visit the king in his blindness. They should not provide him with food, help, money or drinks in his bad condition. The Igwe Onowu suffered terribly and later died. The king died in abject poverty and sickness. The people buried him without the glamour and royal rituals that accompanied such monarchs. He really died unsung. The deity later ordered that no one from the king's village Ibelenta should be crowned a king in Atani any longer. No kings should come out from that village again. The other villages should rotate the crown among themselves and never include Ibelenta. That order had remained in force since then. This is the origin of the saying in Atani that ***Ibelenta adiro echi eze*** implying that Ibelenta village does not produce kings.

COMMENTS

This looks like a legend or history. It is an explanation that the decrees by gods are never revoked in Igbo land.

i.   Most traditional practices are explained in terms of decrees from the divine and no one can question it.

ii.   .Despotism among leaders should be discountenanced, as it might be a disaster that could affect a whole community. The whole Ibelenta had lost the chance to provide a monarch because of the fault of one man.

iii. Igbo monarchical system is not a hereditary factor. No absolute monarchy in any part of Igboland. It is a constitutional and elected king.

iv.   Leadership of a community does not make a man bigger than any other person within the community.

8.2   Akamkpisi Village loses Agukwu-Nri Stool.
(From Nri, Northwest Igbo Subculture Area)

When Eze-Nri, the King of the Holy City of Nri, established his kingdom, the Akamkpisi village had the exclusive right to be producing the candidate for the highly revered office.   Later, the village lost the right to provide candidates for the office and the other villages took over the privilege. An incident that happened long time ago led to the persistence of this tradition now in Nri.

The Eze Nri was a Holy King who did not work at all. His subjects provided him with food and shelter. He lived on the contributions and offerings of his people. It was a mandate that the subjects should provide their King with food and shelter. The *Adama*, who was the Chief Priest and the highest religious official in the palace, was expected to organise and arrange the system of contribution and collection of the provision for the maintenance of the Holy King. The order should remain in force.

One of the kings came from Akamkpisi in the distant past. His subjects did not like him. They therefore did not provide him with regular supply of food, clothing and other needs. The King suffered several depressions and frustrations as a result of poor maintenance by his subjects. He suffered a lot of hunger and deprivation. His nephew from Obeagu village who noticed that his uncle was not being cared for in the right way, decided to take up the challenge to look after the King. The supply did not go far enough even though it was a good demonstration of his commitment to the royal family.

When the King was about to die, he made a small will on his deathbed. He called his nephew from Obeagu who looked after him and gave him the Royal Insignia of *Ofo,* a ritual staff of power depicting honesty and authority. The *Ofo staff* of office was the highest symbol of authority in the whole Igboland. The king made a will that from that day he gave the Ofo to a man from Obeagu, Akamkpisi would never smell the kingship any more. No sooner he gave the Ofo to his nephew from Obeagu than the king died. The kingship there and then shifted to Obeagu and ceased to be given to any one from any other village. Chukwu approved the will and confirmed the stay of the Ofo in Obeagu. This annoyed men from Akamkpisi. They made many overtures to regain their rights as producers of the Royal Monarch. They consulted an oracle who advised them not to embark on any war at all. They later decided to withdraw from war since Chukwu was against it. The Adama, acting on the wise counsel of Chukwu informed them not to engage in war against Obeagu, as that would cause a big loss in human and material resources. Many other villages began to support Obeagu for taking over the royal office. From that day, the right to produce the King went over to other villages. The treatment given to a King is very important in Igbo traditional society and any act of disrespect was viewed with seriousness. Since that time, the people had learnt to respect their king and no one from Akamkpisi had ever been chosen again as a royal father.

COMMENTS

The Nri-Kingship is shrouded in mystery. Most of it is still not easily explicable. There is a lot of internal struggle even in the recent past over this long established awe-inspiring royal throne. There had been threats of secession of one village from the entire clan. Although the Eze-Nri is regarded as divine, no clan worships him as god. The Igbo do not worship their kings or elders, yet they respect them. The early European Anthropologists daubed the religion Ancestor Worship- a wrong terminology which many learned indigenous Africans have challenged and corrected.

The myth also underscores the importance of care of the elderly in Igbo society. It is an abomination for one not to care for one's parents or relatives. It is a source of blessing to care of one's old parents and a curse to neglect them. In preliterate society, when writing was not popular, Oral Sayings like Wills, Prayers, were honoured and valid documents. The Oral Will made by the Eze-Nri remained in force.

CHAPTER NINE
IGBO MARKETS

9.1 Origin of Igbo Markets.
(Version from Ibagwa- Aka, North Igbo subculture Area)

In Ibagwa, near Nsukka, in the distant past, no one knew anything about markets. People depended on what they produced and lived on them. If anyone needed any other thing, he could either consult a neighbour or look for a close relative to supply him with his needs. It was a close society where everyone knew each other and there was no contact with people from other unknown parts of the world then. As a small closed society, people did not travel wide either. So it was a microcosmic world and people lived within their enclave.

A very intelligent and hard working lady, called Lolu Asaju had a rich harvest from her farm. She used to give out many things to those around her and even extended to those in the next village. She was known for here kindness. One day, she came out with a lot of things-vegetable, yam, okro, and cocoyam, in big baskets and displayed in a very wide and open space for passers-by and neighbours to see and pick up some of the things they might need. She did it for two days and many people came out to her display venue and collected some of the things they needed. She began by giving out some of the wares free to those who needed them. Later she asked them to exchange what they had with what they needed. Lolu Asadu who used the Amaebo Village square for the display of the goods encouraged some of the women in the village to bring out some of their own wares and join her. Gradually three women joined her for three consecutive days. After a week, the number increased to about twelve women who brought out things for people to come and pick in exchange of what they needed. Many who came invariably liked the way the things were exchanged and enjoyed the social interactions and jokes.   As more people came out to see what was displayed, they also brought out some of their own wares. Those who had nothing to exchange came out merely to ask for the things they needed from those who had them and promised to give them back something in exchange some other time.

The men in the village decided to put up a shed for the women to protect them from hot sun and rain. Gradually many families put up sheds to protect the women who gathered in the Amaebo Square. When people from the neighbouring towns heard what was going on, they visited the square and collected a few things. The next day, they brought some wares to exchange as well. Men who came stayed in one of the sheds and had drinks and exchanged jokes.

It was on Nkwo Day that Lolu Asadu brought out her wares for the first time.   That made the Ibagwa people call the centre Nkwo Ibagwa. Later, the elders of the community decided to build a shrine there at Nkwo and called it **Onu Nkwo**- meaning the *Mouth of Nkwo*. This was to attract the town deity close to the centre to offer protection to those who come to the Nkwo Ibagwa to exchange goods. Many people from other parts of Nsukka and Igboland began to go to Nkwo Ibagwa to look for what ever they needed to give out or collect from those who have them. When money economy was introduced, people began to give and take money in exchange of goods. As time went on, the deity decided that it would be only on Nkwo Day that people should assemble at the square for exchange of goods. That day became dedicated to the deity. From the daily meeting and gathering, the market developed and later turned to be held once in every four days. That was once a week in Igbo traditional calendar of four-day week. Women and men became regular visitors to the square on Nkwo Day. Those who had nothing to sell went out to the market just for sight seeing and relaxation with friends and those who have something to sell or buy met there as well.

COMMENTS

The myth underscores barter as the original way of economic exchange before money economy. Exchange of goods is better done in the open than in a hidden or obscure place. The need for markets is another pointer to Igbo communal way of existence. No Igbo can successfully live without the support and interaction with others. So communalism has been a way of inter-personal and communal relationship.

i.   Women are more attracted to the market than men. Naturally, Igbo men who have nothing to do in the market occasionally visit it just for the fun of it. It is those who have something to sell or buy that go to markets. Women have natural flare for visiting markets even if it is to buy a cup of salt or a box of match.

ii. Gods are associated with Igbo markets. Each market in Igbo market is dedicated to the protection of a patron deity. As the scale extended, the deities protected distant travellers to the markets. The number of distant visitors to a market enhanced the fame of the community and developed its economy.

iii. The Igbo are celebrated travellers, making their living wherever they sojourn and contribute immensely to the development of the communities where they found themselves.

Many markets hold once a week to allow other communities hold theirs. It encouraged friendship and mutual understanding for people from one village to attend the markets of the other villages.

Such enhanced inter-village friendships and economic co-operation. No one village monopolised the idea of a market in Igbo society.

9.2   The Igbo Market Days- and Igbo Traditional Calendar

The Igbo Calendar took its origin from Nri. In the beginning, the days of the week had no names. Chukwu did not give names to the days of the week when he was supplying food to Eri and later to Nri. Although markets had existed in many communities, none of them had a name. This was because there was no way to count the days because the sun was shining without setting. Besides, no one slept because there no was night.

Four travellers arrived at Aguleri, the ancestral home of the Umunri people. The Umunri people migrated from Aguleri to Oraeri and that is why the Eze-Nri had to go on pilgrimage to Aguleri as a part of the consecration and ritual ceremony. The four visitors were on their way to a market. Each of them carried smoked fish to sell in the market. They were fish merchants. They got tired after a day's long trek. There was no hotel for travellers. The four merchants went to the house of Nri and asked to be allowed to spend the night there. Igbo traditional customary hospitality made it necessary for Nri to offer hospitality to those stranded visitors from a distant town. That time, Nri was still living at Aguleri.

Nri asked Chukwu through his oracular priest the names of the four visitors and where they came from. Chukwu did not give him any answer but promised that he would give him somebody who would disclose the names of the visitors. Little did Nri know that the visitors were spirits or deities from the Spirit World who posed like merchants. They carried fish and it was *Azu Igwe* that Chukwu fed Eri in the earliest time when he sent him to the earth. When the food supply ran out after Eri's death, Nri petitioned Chukwu to send him food. So Nri had been very close to Chukwu and serious in all his negotiations with Chukwu.

Chukwu sent one wise man who was called Okpete to help Nri ascertain the names of the guests in his home. Okpete came to Nri's home with his rat- (oke), which was one of his instrumental agents of divination. On his arrival, Okpete made the sun to set and darkness fell. The visitors could not see again. They were tired and began to shut their eyes as they began to dose off. Within a short time, they slept off as a result of the darkness. They were called up to eat and after the entertainment, they went back to the room, which Nri gave them to spend the night.

When everyone in the house slept off, Okpete brought out his intelligent rat and tied a long rope at its waist. He let the rat off into the fish baskets of the visitors. When the rat got into the basket of the **first** of the unknown visitors **(ndi na onweghi onye malu afa fa- people whose names were unknown),** one of his companions called him by name- **Eke! Eke!**, to warn him that something was trying to tear open his basket of fish. Okpete immediately took notice of the one called Eke and withdrew his rat. When everyone seemed to be asleep again, he released the rat again and this time to another basket. One of the companions woke him up and called him by his name- **Oye! Oye! (Orie, Orie**), and informed him to check whether his basket was properly tied as there seemed to be something attempting to open it. This time again, Okpete noted the one addressed as **Oye** and withdrew his smart rat. Thus Okpete continued till he got to the baskets of the four visitors and got their names as their colleagues called them. The last two were called **Afo** and **Nkwo** respectively.

In the morning, Okpete left before the visitors got up and disclosed the names to Nri. When the visitors came out to wash their faces before leaving, Nri called and greeted them by their names *Eke, Oye, Afo and Nkwo*. This surprised them. They saw Nri as a very wise man. They left and established the four Igbo markets in the town where they sold their fish to the people who came to buy food. Since that time, the rat has been attracted to smoked fish and no one is allowed to keep fish at a place where rats can eat them up at night. The Igbo four-day market week began that day. The four divine visitors rewarded Nri with the gift of naming the four markets after them. This was their special gift to Nri for his hospitality. They blessed him and asked him to make use of the markets as a source of economic development. That is why many people from that part of Nri area-particularly the present Anambra State are the most widely travelled businessmen in Nigeria as well as the highest importers of foreign goods.

The four men did not return to Aguleri again. Nri later discovered that the men were gods. The four market days from that day began to be associated with gods. Throughout Igboland, Eke, is the first day of the Igbo week (Izu) and the most sacred day when nothing like burial should be conducted. Many people born on Eke Day are regarded as people born on holy days.

COMMENTS

It is still amazing that the four Igbo market days are known by the common name that are in use in all the identifiable subculture areas. These are the four names in use in the traditional calendar in Igboland and this calendar is a factor of unity in Igbo world.

i.   *Ndi-Igbo* believe that it is Chukwu who sent the four visitors to come and establish the market as source of economic livelihood. Markets become sacred institution in Igbo economy and no one attempts to harm travellers to the market. It is the moral duty of the king or leader of any community to protect people travelling from other towns to the market in his own domain. Visitors on a market trip to a town have immunity and should not be attacked by thieves, slave raiders, or warriors and head-hunters. It is an abomination to attack women or men on the way to and from market.

ii.   It is always good to show hospitality and kindness to visitors- The Igbo are good at that as it might be an indirect way to show kindness to a deity or spirit that in turn bring blessings.

iii. Wisdom is important in determining even the secrets of the gods. The Igbo believe that with wisdom and purity as well as strong charms, one can decipher the minds of the gods.

iv.   The Igbo believe that humans have responsibility and contribution in the management of created universe. Humans gave names to some of the created God gave man that power.

CHAPTER TEN
CHUKWU AND HUMAN CONDITIONS

10.1.   Skin Differentiation and Colour Pigmentation
(Version from Old Umuahia, South Igbo Subculture Area)

When *Okaka* (The Great God) was creating humans, he came to a stage
– the final one- which was baking the human figure he made from clay on
a very hot oven he made. The clay pot in Igboland is still fired properly
to make them strong and resistant to contain water without leaking. He
put humans on the kiln made of firewood and put fire under the heap of
wood. He went out briefly to pick up an instrument in one of his rooms.
The one below was the first person he put on the firewood before he lit
the fire underneath. The one on top was the second person he put on
the fire and it was on top of the first man. When he came back, the one
below, placed directly on the wood had gone very dark as a result of
excess heat. The one on top came out bright, lustre and sparking because
of less heat on its skin.   The one below was the first person he made and
his skin turned out to be completely dark from the smoke of the fire.
When Chukwu eventually brought out the two people, he saw that the
one below was darker than the one on top. The one whose body was
closer to the source of heat became permanently black while the one on
top, became lighter and brighter.   Thus the skins of the two people
became dark and light and they became the ancestors of the Black and
White races respectively.

COMMENTS:

i. the black race still claims to be the first to be created- the Primacy of African Humanity

ii. the age of created things in Igbo society can be determined by their skin coloration- eg fruits tend to be lighter when in the second stage of maturity or decomposition.

iii. Chukwu did not make mistake but chose to bring out the objects as he planned. The Igbo do not believe that Chukwu made mistake in creation;

iv. The idea of being on top of the other has been taken to imply suppression and oppression as evidenced by the suffering of the Blacks in the hands of white colonial administrators and hitherto in many parts of the world. The man on top oppresses the one below.

v. The Black was equipped to withstand heat and hence can work under the scotching heat of the sun while the whites cannot work under the intense heat of the sun.

vi. Black bones are stronger because of vitamin D they get from the sun and can carry heavy burden on both head and shoulders.

vii. This underscores in a subtle way the problem of Time. Those who attend appointments early choose the better part of the booty and sit anywhere they choose. Does this account for Igbo lack of concept of punctuality in time management.

10.2 Skin Differentiation
(Version from Ezihe Mbano, Isu- Ama Subunit of South Igbo Culture Area)

When Chukwu created human beings, everyone was black. The clay was dark and human figures Chukwu made from it were dark. Later Chukwu decided to make the skin colour of the black figures a little lighter. He placed a very big pot at a corner and filled it with water. He ordered two men to go to the pot early in the morning and bathe with the water in it. One of the men came out early enough and used the whole water in the pot and washed his whole body, legs, hands, trunk, neck, armpit, hands, everywhere. The other man came late after the first man had used up all the water. There was not enough water again in the pot for the second man. He put his palms, sole of his feet, and rinsed his mouth. Thereafter he left in anger.

When both men went to the sun to dry their body, the man who had his whole body washed turned out to be lighter and could not resist the heat of the sun. The other man who washed only the sole of his feet, his palms, and rinsed his mouth was darkened by the heat, which he enjoyed. Since that day, the man who washed his whole body became the ancestor of the white people while the other became the ancestor of the black people who had only their palms, soles of their feet and their mouth lighter than their main trunk. His other unwashed part of the body did not get lighter skin again. Since that day, the black man has been washing his body regularly wherever he saw water to see if he could get a little lighter that he was. He later gave up when he saw that it was useless to struggle to change the colour of his skin. Since that day, the black man would like to wash up to five times a day whenever he sees water whether it is cold or warm. He began to enjoy the sun and thought that it would help him change the skin colour. The white man does not like to wash his body as often as the black man does because he thinks he is white enough and fears the sun because he suspected it will make his skin darker again.

COMMENTS

i.   The Igbo still believe that Black is the original colour of humans when Chukwu created them.

ii.   Any fresh fruit is said to be 'black' if it is not yet ripe or mature for eating. For instance mango or banana is black or green but gets lighter or white when it is about to be eaten. The light skinned people were those who were created later.

iii.   That Chukwu did not give the skin pigmentation immediately does not suggest that Chukwu made mistake in creation .It does not presuppose mutation or evolutionary trends in Igbo creative cosmogony

iv.   The Igbo are fast moving people who detest lateness in any appointment. Often some foreign anthropologists and ethnographers describe them as people without patience. Yet they are patient and prepared to wait if they know that they are not waiting in vain. They are punctual at any function as to be able to get the fresh part of any provision that will be distributed. Hence there is an Igbo adage that **Anu bu uzo na anu mmiri oma** – meaning that it is the animal that comes to the spring first that drinks the fresh water that comes out. Their punctuality in business may be a reflection of their name **IGBO**- often interpreted to mean: **I Go Before Others.** Their promptness in standing out first in every human endeavour has earned them a lot of hatred from many other ethnic nationalities in the world. Hence their detractors accuse them of inordinate ambition, greed and over acquisitiveness. Yet they are hardworking and self-reliant and never see hard work as a vice. While others revel in luxury, the Igbo spend their time working and struggling for success. Hence it is an achievement-oriented society.

10.3 Differences in Human Complexion
(Version from Ezza, Abakaliki, Northeast Igbo Subculture Area)

In the distant past, Chukwu wanted to create human beings after he had created all other things in the universe. He created a man and a woman. He asked the man to marry the woman and both of them lived as husband and wife. They looked very beautiful and elegant. Chukwu was happy to see them look good and strong. When he spoke to them, they responded and this gladdened Chukwu's heart. He asked them not to move out too far from the beautiful compound he lived with them. The man had a very long nose. His wife also had a long nose. That day, the sun was not shining. The weather was cool and Chukwu asked the man and his wife to stay indoors or in a cool shade

Later the sun came out and saw the beautiful work Chukwu had made. He went close to them and his presence hardened their bodies and darkened them. Their pointed nose became shortened and broadened. The man and his wife became very hard and strong and turned black because of the sun's close visit to them.

Chukwu created another couple the next day since the first batch of man and woman was a good work. He brought out his clay and began the work of moulding again. When he had finished putting the shape in order, he placed the figures – male and female – in another shade, The Sun did not see the second beautiful work their Master (Chukwu) had produced again. This sun did not come very close to this new set. They remained in the cool shed for a long time and it took time before they got properly dry. Later when they were brought, they did not see the sun that had gone away. The pointed nose of this second set of couple remained in tact. Their body remained bright and soft. When Chukwu later asked the Sun why he came out to disturb his first creatures, the sun apologised and promised that he would from that day take care of the couple by providing them with warmth, light, and making sure that they remain strong and have strong bodies, bones and good hard food. The other couple did not get the same benefits from the sun like the first couple. Chukwu sent them out to a far place where the sun scarcely gets to them. They lived in extreme cold, never smiled, and never visited each other.

They locked themselves in shed and huts trying to keep warm by whatever covering they could find. Whenever they came out to work or play outside, they enjoyed the rays of the sun and its light and warmth which made them smile to one another and exchange greetings with friends and neighbours. They became the ancestors of the Black Race who are friendly, warm, cheerful and strong. The other couple became the ancestors of the white people who are a bit withdrawn, individualistic, locked up, gloomy and shaking with cold every time, soft bones, and when they came to the sun, they go out burnt. Today, many Black have resisted the heat of the sun while the white skinned people fear excess heat. Even in wet season, the Sun would come out to check whether the Igbo are warm enough. He made the promise to Chukwu that he would look after the Igbo at all times. The Igbo in appreciation of the benevolence of the Sun, established a Cult for him and today there are people who worship the Sun as a deity of cheerfulness and bright nature and success. May your sun shine for ever is a blessing people give to those they love May your sun never set is a wish and pray of long life for people.

COMMENTS.

i. The myth still upholds the primacy of the Black as the original humanity.

ii. the cult of the Sun is firmly established in many parts of the Igbo world

iii. Often people equate the Sun with Chukwu and answer the Sun as names e.g.

Anyanwu-	Sun
Anyanwu Oma-	God sun
Anyanwu emeka -	The sun has blessed me
Nwanyanwu--	son of the Sun
Eke-Anyanwu-	the sun that creates

Although people in some culture Igbo areas interchange names for God (Chukwu) with Anyanwu (Sun) they do not confuse them.

iv.   The presence of the sun in Igbo world has brought a lot of advantages: food production, health care and general disposition of people. They Igbo describe a pretty girl as Anyanwu- Ututu- Morning rays of the Sun.

In all, the myth endorses the fact that the creation of humans of different skin pigmentation was an act of divine design and not an accident. Chukwu never regretted that the added colours to the leaves, trees, animals, humans, the earth surface, the sky, the rainbows, seas, etc. All were in his master plan and not a product of accidental results.

APPENDICES

DIVINE KINGSHIP AND POLITICAL RITUALS AMONG THE IGBO

There are numerous accounts of legendary monarchies in West Africa. The Edo, Yoruba, Ashanti and Efik, for instance are among the popular powerful kingdoms whose histories still refer to serious encounters with colonial administration. There are accounts of serious wars between some of those kings and European administrators. Meyerowitz describes the Ashanti King as a 'sacred ruler of a sacred State'

Among the Yoruba, the Alafin of Oyo is believed to be the direct progeny of the legendary and semi-divine Oduduwa, the mythical founder of the Yoruba Kingdom. The Oni of Ife is also believed to be the son of the Oduduwa the Creator of the Yoruba known Universe. The early Portuguese missionaries to Benin found a well –established and organised kingdom ruled by a monarch who was so powerful that when they took the news to King John II of Portugal (1481 – 1495), he sought to open a friendly correspondence and contact with the Benin Monarch. They saw the Oba of Benin, as one who occupied a higher post in his domain than the Pope did in Catholic Europe, because he was seen by his subjects not only as God's vice-regent on earth but also as a god himself.

The early writers had not credited the Igbo with such rulers with mythical or legendry powers and influence. The case of Nri is at best described as a '*society with a specialised caste of priests'*. The Obi of Onitsha is acclaimed divine by his subjects. Yet C.K Meek, in spite of a long and brilliant investigation into Onitsha political system described the Obi (King of Onitsha) not so much as a King than as the president of a bureaucratic society. What an insult and error of judgement! The monarchs from other parts of Africa described, as kings did not have as much influence as the Onitsha King.

R.N. Henderson saw Onitsha as an instance of a highly centralised state, unlike other Igbo societies. He could not state specifically whether the Obi had a divine origin or not. Yet the Monarch, the Nri and Onitsha Kingship had been in existence long before the Igbo contact with Europeans. They were models of Igbo political and royal leadership built on Igbo traditional worldview and concept of Power. The Igbo model or concept of Kingship should not conform to any other model before it is recognised by non-Igbo people, no matter their index of assessment. That would be external imposition on Igbo worldview. Many other Igbo communities have in the recent past started to pattern the leadership of their places along the lines of established 'chiefdom' that is not hereditary in order not to destroy the traditional Igbo republican nature.

Onitsha people see their Obi as both Divine and Sacred. The Nri Kingship which had existed for almost 10,000 years is also regarded as 'divine' because the Igbo like other Africans are highly religious people whose life is primarily entrenched in their religion. Every aspect of life is under the influence and control of Religion. There are no atheists, agnostics, freethinkers or secular humanists in African societies in general and Igbo society in particular.

APPENDIX A
The Divine Umunri King

The origin of this peculiar institution is traceable to one of the Igbo myths of creation about a legendry founding father, Eri, of the Igbo people. It is an ancient kingdom traceable to prehistoric times. Chukwu sent down Eri from the Sky when he created the solid earth. The descendants of the royal families lived in Agukwu and claimed ancestry to Eri. They called themselves UMUNRI- the children of Nri, who happened to be the youngest of the four sons of Eri- the first created man to sojourn the earth. This is where the Igbo King of Nri claims that it is divine and ancient. The traditions of the 'divine monarch' are mixed with myth and history and it is difficult to distinguish one from the other. This is where its divine origin hinges as it is beyond human ability to trace its origin with certainty and clarity. It is only the Divine Beings who created the Royal Institution and maintained it with sanctions and rituals.

M.J.D Jeffrey's work on the Umunri people whom he called **Umundri** traced the origin of their kingship outside Igboland. He contended that the people of Nri came from the ruling stock of the Igala and thus connected them with the Atta of Igala. Yet in the Igbo myth of origin, it was a stock of the Nri under Onoju, the son of the second wife of Eri who left to establish the Igala Kingdom. Jeffrey supported his claims with the purported ethnographic data of one Captain Clifford of the then colonial Nigerian Civil Service who surveyed Kingship among the Igala.[1]

He thought that the Umunri people who though spoke Igbo today and no other local language, were not Igbo at all but might have settled among the people whom they called the **IGBO.** However, Igala Oral traditions state that the second wife of Eri called Oboli bore Onuju who left the Anambra River basin and became one of the founders of Igalaland.[2] So Igala Kingship descended from Eri who bore Nri who founded the Umunri people. The Atta of Igala was of the Eri stock and had Igbo origin. Most names of the Igala people look similar to the Igbo e.g., **Onwe, Ochefu, Ukpabi, Obi, Okweche**, although they have different meanings and sounds in Igala. The Igbo of Nsukka influenced the Idah so much that the place still has links with the Igbo with whom they share many things in common- e.g. markets, patterns of dressing, inter-marriage, etc.

There is a version of the Nri traditions of origin collected around Enugwu- Agidi and Nawfia which states that the people first settled around **OLI NRI** stream very close to Onitsha from where they moved to Aguleri and finally to Agukwu-Nri. At Agukwu, they cleared part of the thick forest from which the present town got its name- **Agukwu**- Big Forest.

Okoye Aniezue, an elder from Enugu –Agidi, stated that Nri after settling in the new place, had some internal dissension and a part of Agukwu seceded to found the town **of Oraeri** with its own 'divine king'. In Thurston Shaw's description of the excavations in Igboland, he tries to connect what looked like the grave of a divine-king or priest –king with the institution of this Eze-Nri, although he was cautiously non-specific and conclusive on whether there was any such connection or not. He opined that 'it was inviting to associate the finds at Igbo-Ukwu with the institution of Eze-Nri, the priest –king of the Umunri Clan of the Ibos…' and stopped short at that.[3]

It is at Agukwu- Nri that the highest order of priesthood is said to exist because it is there that the religious headquarters was established before the secession and movement towards Ora-eri. The Adama- Chief Priest – and his associates became great travellers and possibly could have spread some aspects of kingship to Igala, Bini, Yoruba and other non-

Igbo groups with whom they came into contact during the period dating far back into history before the colonial days. They spread their influence to other Igbo groups as medicine men, (dibia) smiths, purveyors of cult and civilization, circumcisers, and ritual specialists removing abominations in compounds and communities. They hold the oldest and highest Ofo – Staff of Authority- which confers on them the authority to become ritual experts. Hence, every Nri man is regarded as a priest everywhere he sojourns - (**Umuoje na Mmuo**- travellers to the Spirit world).

The ruler of the town who is called the Eze-Nri (King of Nri) is the supposed holder of the highest Ofo staff in Igbo land. The Eze-Nri on assumption of office, after his coronation, is transformed into a god. The Eze-Nri himself is not a priest and does not offer sacrifice since his divine nature gave him a much higher status than the rank of a priest. The Adama was responsible for the ceremony that transforms the candidate for the high office of Eze-Nri into a 'god'. This is a ceremony that lasts for more than one year. It was after the group had settled that the Adama crowned the first Eze-Nri.

After the **death** of the Eze-Nri, there is usually an inter-regnum of seven years before a new king is crowned. During the inter-regnum, the gods would make clear the candidate of their choice and no one would be in doubt of the person. The Eze-Nri does not **die** because he becomes a **god** as soon as he is crowned. He rather joins his ancestors or goes on a pilgrimage because as a god, he will not die. In his temporary absence (seven years of interregnum), the Adama performs the palace duties until the Eze-Nri returns. This means the Adama will be in control of palace duties until a new Eze-Nri is crowned. A chosen candidate for the high office is made known to the people by the gods. He may show signs of his choice in several ways, among which is a demonstration of the ability to prophesy that which must surely come true. The candidate then makes sacrifices at all the shrines in the town and pays some fees to the Adama.

It is the Adama who controls the royal regalia and directs the ceremony that transforms the candidate into a god.

On the day the new Eze-Nri will be transformed into a god, implying the day he will be crowned, he will be prepared like a corpse and buried in a shallow grave. His *funeral ceremony* is performed and his wives mourn him. His humanity is dead and he will never die again when he becomes the Eze-Nri because he becomes a god as soon as the crowning is completed. At sunset, the buried candidate is exhumed from the grave and his body is replaced with a banana stem and his corpse is carried outside the compound to which he will never again return. The corpse is then washed clean with water from a sacred lake and placed on a cowhide (akpukpo anu efi). Thereafter the body is smeared with Nzu (white chalk) throughout and may be touched by only the Adama, a female dwarf (Akanshi) or a virgin. He is regarded as the protector of the oppressed.

The oldest wife of the candidate (Queen of the Eze-Nri to be), is also whitened and she like her husband discards her usual dress for a white locally –woven cloth like the Akwette or Uburu or Kente cloth. The King-elect adds copper anklets (nkwuli) to his regalia in order to insulate himself from the pollution of the world around while his Lolo (queen) covers her head with white head tie.

Soon after this stage, the royal couple accompanied by the dwarf, (usually referred to as their child), the Adama representatives and a large retinue, move to Aguleri, on a very long journey. The journey to Aguleri is significant because it is said to be their traditional home before they migrated to Agukwu. Besides, the King-elect is greeted with rejoicing and praises at any town he passes through.

At Ukpo, in Njikoka, the Eze-Nri-elect climbs a special white ant-hill and prays to Chukwu, the Supreme God, and other ancestors, who were supposed to have worshipped Chukwu at that holy – hill. When he gets to Aguleri, the Eze-Nri elect sits on a heap of stones in the public square where many people would gather to see him. He eats part of the Nzu (the white chalk) with which his body was whitened. This symbolises an immortal life and his admittance into the fellowship of Anyanwu- the Sun god whom he represents. He is believed to be a righteous king, pure, spotless and immortal. He then recreates the world, thus dividing the waters of the Anambra River. In other words, he calms the river and forces all the animals of the sea to depart in order to allow an Aguleri man to pick the *Ududu,* important royal regalia, from the bed of the sea. It is the Aguleri man who presents this royal regalia to the Eze-Nri, an indication of their royal blood connection before the movement to Agukwu.

From Aguleri, the royal train returns home. Four days after the return from the Holy Pilgrimage to Aguleri, the Eze-Nri causes a palm tree to flower and fruit and the fruit to ripen, all in one day. This is a demonstration of mystical and spiritual power and might on the part of the New Eze-Nri who would be living with his Lolo (the Queen) in a palm frond booth. During the interim, he would be waiting for his coronation. While he is waiting, the town's people build a royal palace for the new King- Eze-Nri-.

The Eze-Nri will not be crowned until the community completes the new palace for him. On his way to the palace to be crowned, the Eze Nri elect is set upon by the Queen whom he overcomes and puts down. The queen in return, attacks the Eze Nri and overcomes him too. This is arranged as a mock battle to put away any pollution that might follow should any of them fall while quarrelling or fighting at home when they enter the palace. Besides, a ritual fight in which the king attacks and defeats a young man, and also an old man follows this. His victory of both of them presents him a gallant warrior who would be able to defend his subjects in future in case the town is attacked. He is supposed to be a gallant warrior who overcomes every enemy.

He arrives at the palace, which is not walled yet. He mounts the throne, which is made of an earth mound in which the skull of the former Eze-Nri was buried. He sits on a cowhide or a special stool, which is exclusively reserved for the King. The stool has one leg which branches into three, just like a tripod stand. Many other royal regalia are placed near the throne in front of the King. These include, the Ofo, sacred staff of office, sacred spear- (Ube or Aro Ozo), and the Ududu, which he collected at Aguleri during the Pilgrimage. The Adama or his representative also puts a cowhide crown adorned with eight feathers on the head of the Eze-Nri. The number eight is symbolic of the Igbo market days and week. The four- day week is the 'small week' – (Izu Nta) and the eight-day week (is big week) - Izu Ukwu. This means that every day in the week, all year round, throughout life, the Eze Nri is protected from any attack of the enemy and he is in control of any situation. Every day is in the hands of the Eze Nri. The Divine King is the Controller of all events all year round, through out life in the whole world- the Igbo known world.

He sits on the throne for twelve days following the coronation and receives delegates and official dignitaries from other communities and societies who come to pay him homage and courtesy call as he accedes to the throne and assumes both political power and spiritual authority.   The Eze Nri is thus crowned- and shouts of ***Eze-Nri echie! Eze Nri echie*** fill the whole place

In conclusion, we must state that one of the greatest events in Igboland is the development of Nri Civilization, which can be described as the civilization of the 'Sacred and Divine Institution'. The Eze-Nri who derives his legitimacy and authority from Chukwu (God) lays emphasis on ***Peace- Udo***-. It was a Kingdom in which both political and economic systems were highly ritualised. For instance, as some of the myths have highlighted, trading activities were associated with ritual markets called, ***Eke, Oye (Orie), Afo, and Nkwo*** and this was spread through out the Igbo world as Nri itinerant ritual experts sojourned.

Agricultural produce, yam, cocoyam, palm produce, and vegetables were ritualised in the *Ifejioku (Ahianjoku, Ohanjoku or Afianjoku)* cults. The Eze-Nri, symbolized Peace, a figure who held absolute authority and power, which did not corrupt. No wonder people of the community regarded him as 'Divine'. He was a King whose ethical philosophy and religious dogma rejected slave trade, because it involved shedding of blood which Nri regarded as an abomination.[4] It was a Kingdom that did not colonise the neighbouring communities but rather went out to share with them ritual food and cults. It was a kingdom whose interest was on helping and developing others instead of enriching itself by exploiting and oppressing them.

However western anthropologists, culture historians and ethnographers understood and interpreted Nri Hegemony, it was one in which leadership was ritualised in the various title systems epitomized in Ozo-title controlled and directed by the Eze-Nri and his Adama- the Chief Priest. It is a sort of Theocracy rather than Democracy.

APPENDIX B
The Ofala in Onitsha: The Festival of a Sacred King

The Obi (King) of Onitsha is a very highly respected monarch and divine personality. His subjects regard him as a divine personality who is without blemish and cannot sin. He is supposed to have no emotions and always poses as one without them. Any one who is a descendant of the royal family *(Umu Ezechima)* on his father's side may be elected king. Obi-elect undergoes a period of *Iche Ndo*, known as regency and purification. Thereafter, he is crowned. The Obi never leaves his palace and is rarely seen more than once a year in public except during the *Ofala Festival*. In other words, he stays in the palace, praying for the people, ordering their lives, ruling them with the council, and administers the entire community.

The Obi performs certain rituals and observes some taboos. These enhance his spiritual power and protect him from pollution and diminution of his spiritual force that he uses to run the Kingdom. These are some of the taboos. The Obi should not cry at all. He does not and should not see his mother if she were still alive. He would not see the River Niger, the Otumoye Lake and a corpse. He does not cross a river, should not sleep outside his palace meaning he should not spend the night outside the town. He does not dance at all except at the Ofala Festival when he performs a ritual dance with his chiefs. He does not eat in the presence of any body except his special assistants (servants). He does not eat food prepared by anyone who is not a virgin.

Many Igbo communities have started to reinterpret the social and religious significance of their annual festivals and traditional leadership to reflect their new politico- religious consciousness. They are looking at things that can bring otherwise atomistic little kindred and sub clans into a big and united town. The Onitsha model has attracted many Igbo communities where republicanism had prevailed for centuries. Since microcosmic worldview is giving way to a macro world and extension of scale, development could be more easily enhanced when many previously independent units come together with their resources to embark on long-term projects.

Ofala Festival in Onitsha falls within the period of New Yam Festival in many other Igbo communities and towns. Consequently, many young and successful businessmen and women who live in urban cities and some who live in **Diaspora** think that Ofala in Onitsha is a New Yam Festival. Some people have, therefore, begun to rename the New Yam Festival in their community the Ofala Festival. Their aim is to have a central annual festival that would be a rallying point for the town to meet and talk of socio-economic and political development.

This new way of thinking is gaining grounds in many Igbo societies with the newly introduced system of Chieftaincy Institutions. The word Ofala is not quite easy to explain in Igbo land. One of the officials in the Obi's palace who is well –educated in the traditions of his people   gave us two possible interpretations. His analysis is quite beyond what many people know about the festival. The curiosity to analyse the meaning of the word OFALA is current. It is people with academic interest who posed the questions to some elders who had for life never thought of explaining the meaning of the word.   However we were told that Ofala might mean in the first place, the **OFO ALA**. It indicated the period the Obi strikes the great and revered staff of office Ofo on the ground as ritual prayers for the blessings of the land, the people, and the community. It is a ritual time of prayers with Ofo, on behalf of the people for the blessings received from the deities of the community in the past year.

The elder who is a Palace Chief relates the origin of the festival to the celebration of the victory Obi had over his enemies in war. He also stated that the New Yam was brought into the festival as a later addition, which has in the course of years overshadowed the original historical background and meaning of the celebration, which was victory over enemies during the war. Onitsha people had a very real association and relationship with yam- **Discorea Spp.** Forced by famine to explore every possible avenue for food, the people decided to eat a special type of yam which was until then regarded as poisonous and dangerous. Precautions were taken to avert its supposed harmful effects on people. The smallest kindred in Onitsha was asked by the Obi to eat the yam first. This was to make sure that if it was dangerous, only a handful of people would die and the other parts of the town would live. Hunger was severe and no food was available to the community. Yet this wild crop was found everywhere and no one had learnt how to eat it to make sure that it is good for food.

Following a set course, roasted yam treated with Nn'edi leaves followed by yam pounded into foo-foo, and served with Nsala Soup, (all accompanied with prayers, incantations and offering to the deities and ancestors), many other kindreds tasted the new crop and did not die. The food was therefore recommended as a non-poisonous and edible crop. The species of yam used in this case was called *Ji- Ofia*- Wild Yam- not the type the Igbo got from Chukwu following Nri's petition.

The other version of the story states that the smallest village was asked to taste the new yam which would be used by the Obi and his people to celebrate Obi's victory over his enemy in the past year. The other villages and the Obi himself watched the outcome with interest and fear. If the villagers who ate the new foodstuff died, it would be declared unsuitable for human consumption but if it did them no harm, both the Obi and the other people would join in eating it. The Obi had just won a serious battle over his enemies and would not like to sustain casualties any more by allowing people die after eating a strange poisonous food item. That was why he directed the smallest village should be used as a taste case. The smallest village ate the new yam without fatal consequences. This amazed the Obi and his cabinet who asked the other villages to eat the new yam as well. If nothing fatal happened to them also, the Obi will finally join them in eating the new yam. The day fixed for the Obi to taste the New Yam was called *Iwaji- Eze-* meaning Slicing off or Cutting off the King's own Yam.

The Ofala, which was celebrated as the King's ritual of thanksgiving for his victory in war, would come thirteen days after he had tasted the New Yam. It is this association with the new yam that made people think that Ofala was celebration of the King's tasting of the new yam. A number of rituals precede the Ofala itself. On the eighth day of the IWA-JI, the Obi's diviners called *Ubulu-na- Ikem*, consult the oracle to enquire of the future of the town, the health and life of the Obi, events of the coming year, etc. Thereafter, the Obi would go into a period of retreat (spiritual desert) for about four or five days. This is called *Inye-Ukwu N'uno-* putting legs into the rooms- implying total withdrawal into the rooms and is in total confinement. There in confinement, the Obi communes with the ancestors and performs acts of purification on behalf of himself and of his subjects. He would morn those who died in the previous year. Throughout the period of retreat, the Obi is painted with white chalk- Nzu-. He wears only a white loincloth and a white cap. He will neither bathe nor eat. It is the time of real self-mortification and denial. He will suspend all official palace duties but spends time praying and meditating. He does not receive any visitor, no matter how highly placed, into the palace.

On the Ofala Day proper, the people would throng the palace square where they sing and dance in merriment to welcome or behold the face of Obi who is coming out of the retreat. Each member of the *Ndi Ichie Ume-* the Cabinet Chiefs, who arrives at the palace to pay homage to the Obi, would come with his own musical and dancing group that would herald his arrival. He would dance in the square to the rhythm of his own musical group. As the Obi is about to enter the Palace Square, where thousands of his subjects and invited dignitaries had assembled, the Traditional Prime Minister – the Onowu- would lead the Ndi Ichie to receive him and present him to the public. The climax of the long procession of the Obi and his elders and chiefs comes when the Obi dances to the rhythm of the drums. In the past, every group that moved into the Palace Square toward the Obi would fall on the ground, kneeling down and touching the ground with their foreheads in complete obeisance to the sacred and respected King.

The foodstuff which many people eat is the yam that had been tasted 13 days earlier and it is used in the celebration and entertainment of guests. The *IWAJI EZE*, which came earlier, seemed to have been part of the Ofala as the people remain in festive mood 13 days before the Obi comes out to dance in public as the climax of the Ofala Festival. In effect, the Iwaji Eze had taken place before the Ofala but they seem to be part of the on-going festive mood in the town. New Yam festival is now called Ofala in many Igbo communities, which in its true traditional sense is not what it is in Onitsha.

Notes

1. M.J.D. Jeffreys, The Divine Umudri King. *Africa* 8, 3 (1935). P. 350. See M.D.W. Jeffrey's Divine Umundri King in Igboland. (Ph D. Thesis , University of London, 1934, No. 435, at the SOAS Library)

2. J.S. Boston, *The Igala Kingdom*. Oxford: Oxford University Press, 1968.

3. Thurston Shaw, The Mystery of the Buried Bronze/ Discoveries at Igbo Ukwu, Eastern Nigeria. *Nigeria Magazine*, no. 92(March 967) p. 48

4. M.A. Onwuejeogwu: Evolutionary Trend in the History of the Development of Igbo Civilization. In Ahiajoku Lecture Owerri, 1987, p. 48

5. Marius Nkwo. The Great Ofala, *Nigeria Magazine* no. 110 – 112 (1971) p. 3   See also J. O. Nzekwu, Ofala Festival Nigeria Magazine, no. 16 (1959) pp. 104 – 122 Elizabeth Isichie, Igbo Worlds. London: Macmillan Education Ltd. 1977, pp 139 - 141

CONCLUSION

In this collection, we have attempted to bring together scattered and disorganised tales of wisdom into a comprehensive and coherent body of work. It is a systematic attempt to bring an important aspect of Igbo philosophy and wisdom together for the first time. It is, otherwise, a neglected aspect of Igbo wisdom which people use but have never tried to put them together as found in different parts of Igbo Subculture areas. Far from being the irrelevant and incomprehensible superstition that can be ignored, except for mere entertainment as some people may think or as in the thought of Malinowski, a mere charter for social institutions, myths can be seen in many traditional societies as a key to the understanding of man in his social nature, intellect, imagination, signs and metaphors, his laws and his governments and his historical development. Most of the myths deal primarily with the origin of humans and with the origin of some other social and ritual institutions and practices that account for all life situations.

Although we made several attempts to interpret or comment on the myths, it is an unusual approach to them by the elders who own them. They do not try to explain the myth to anyone. They tell the story and the meaning is understood even if the person is uninitiated. We tried the explanation primarily to help a complete visitor to the people to peer into their epistemology and metaphysics. It is to help young undergraduate students appreciate the amount of wisdom embedded in many African spiritual thoughts. We have not claimed to make infallible explanations but we crosschecked with the real elders and owners of the tales to validate our comments. It is not imposed on their psyche or method of thinking but distilled from it. The explanations do not fully interpret the highly complex cosmology of the African world. Therefore, we have not made any attempt to impose our views on the commentaries we added. The error of imposing ideas on a people's thought-pattern is carefully avoided by the use of Phenomenological and Culture- Area Approach which the author had adopted as a viable methodology in the Study of African Traditional Religion and Culture. African Spirituality benefits from this methodology. Our exegeses and interpretations adhere closely to the traditional elders' own analysis and point of view. In their view, the myths provide the symbolic categories by which they understand and organise their work.

Myths are among the few basic elements that make a people stand out as an independent entity. The language of the tales, the dialect, the vocabulary and the emphasis are obviously indigenous to the people. This quality makes one feel that myths are an aspect of a people's cultural heritage, which is not borrowed. The spiritual image and development which myths nurture give expression of people's understanding of the cosmos. It is not a world void of spiritual power behind the life and work of beings on the universe. The common presence of deities, spirits and gods in many tales underscore people's concepts and idea. How those beings shape life and character, belief and faith, and actions and thought can still be seen in the overall product content of African life.

This first and comprehensive collection of Myths in Igboland will surely stimulate other people to come out with many other myths circulating in different parts of the country dealing with other aspects of life. In all the myths, we did not come across any that explains the end of the world. The Igbo seem to believe that the end of the human world is not enshrined in the plan of the Creator God at the beginning of the world. This life is still a place to act out one's best character and commitment. It does not deny the existence of the spiritual universe but there is not emphasis on the End of Time. In spite of the apparent similarity in many of the versions of same myths from different subculture areas, there is evident mark of originality and peculiarity in each one. That goes to show that each society had its own method of thinking and looking at things.

The traditional religious heritage embedded in Igbo cosmogony still challenges the student of African Spirituality. The complex nature of the religion calls for caution and patience on the part of the scholar. Hasty conclusions should be avoided. The myths do not only preserve the gems of Igbo spirituality and philosophy, they also show that in spite of massive and persistent onslaught by many external agents of change, some core elements of the cultural and religious artefacts have stood the test of time. They have not been preserved in any written form, yet they have persisted and in doing so, offer abiding and lasting scripture of the traditional religion. They are remembered and narrated without difficulty. Questions on the mystery of life in general are still supplied with intelligent and intelligible answers from myths, legends, proverbs, etc. It is important that indigenous African scholars owe it as a duty to assist their people by presenting unadulterated version of the tales and also preserve them as their own contribution to the ongoing quest to document some valuable elements of African heritage.

Finally, one common theme that runs through the myths thus far examined in this study is the tendency for them to evolve a cosmology. They have thus shown common traits of the ability to develop into a kind of theory of explanation of the world and life. This gives the African life a Spiritual focus. By so doing, they have exercised much influence on the way human beings think and act. The ethical implications are therefore overwhelming.

Igbo mythology contains considerable amount of what may be described in modern historiography as 'history'. Invariably, it seems that myths and history generally overlap and become dovetailed into each other.

Myths blend into history as cosmic and analytical events bear upon local situations. In the same way, history blends into myth as local and human events become ritualised and infused with cosmic and analytical meaning. We have illustrated this paradox in the two accounts in Appendices A an B, which deal with political rituals among the Igbo. The two accounts are on the Nri and the Onitsha monarchies, which can be aptly described as Sacred Kings of the people often described as having no kings.

BIBLIOGRAPHY

Abrahamson, H.   The Origin of Death: Studies in African
                        Mythology (Ethnographica Upsalinnsia, 3)
                        Upppsala: Amquist and Wikells

Afigbo, A. E.   Ropes of Sand. Studies in Igbo History and
                        Culture. Nsukka Nigeria U.P.L.   1981. see
                        Chapter 3.

Baumann, H.   Schofung und Urzeit des Menschen im Mythus
                        der Africanischen Volker.
                        Berlin:
                        Dietrich Reimer, 1936. Quoted by E.W. Smith,
                        African Ideas of God, London, 1950

Beir, Ulli,.   The Historical and Psychological Significance of
                        Yoruba Myths. Odu, I,
                        (Jan 1955), pp 17 – 25

------,   The Origin of Life and Death. African Creation
                        Myths. 1966

-------.   The Yoruba Myths. Cambridge. CUP, 1980

Berdyaer, Nicholas.   Freedom and Spirit. (Blas… 1935).

Biobaku, S.   The use and Interpretation of Yoruba Myths.
                        Odu, (1 Jan. 1955)

--------------.   Myths and Oral History Odu. (1 Jan. 1955),
                        pp 12 – 16

Childs, B.S.   Myth and Reality in Old Testament. London
                        S.C,M. 1960

P' Bitek, Okot.   African Religions in Western Scholarship.
                        Nairobi, East African Pub. Co. 970

The Encyclopaedia Americana. Grolier Inc... 1987

Feldmann, Susan   African Myths and Tales. New York. Dell, 1970

Freytag, Walter.   Quoted by M.A.C. Warren. Basilea. Evang.
                        Missions- Verlag. Stuttgart. 1959

Gilesman, M.   Myth and History of African Religion. In T.O. Ranger and I.N. Kimambo (eds) The Historical Study of African Religion. London Heinemann, 972

Griaule, M. & G. Dieterln.   The Dogon of the French Sudan. In D. Forde (ed.) African Worlds. London I.A.I. 1954.

------------.   Convesation with Ogotmmeli. London , Oxford. OUP for I.A.I. , 1965

Hooks, S.H. ed.   Myth, Ritual and Kingship. Oxford Clarendon Press, 1958

Isichie, Elizabeth.   Igbo Worlds. London Macmillian Educational Books, 1977

Jung. Carl. G.   Psychological Reflection: An Anthology of Writings (1953). selected and edited by Jolande Jacobi. New York, Harper , 1961.

Lloyd, P.   Yoruba Myths: A Sociologist's Interpretation. Odu 2 (1955), pp 20 – 22

Long, C.   Oral Literature and Folklore in Africa: A Review Article. History of Religions, 14, 1 (1974) pp 65 – 73

Malonowski, B.   Myth in Primitive Psychology. In B. Malinowski (ed) Magic, Science and Religion and other Essays. New York: Doubleday, 1954

Middleton, John (ed)   Myth and Cosmos. 1967

Okpwho, Isidore.   *Myth in Africa: A study of its aesthetic and cultural relevance*. London: Cambridge University Press. 1983

Parrinder, E.G.   African Mythology. London: Paul Hamlyn. 1967

----------------.   *Dictionary of Non-Christian Religions*. London: Hulton Educational Publishers, 1971

Ray, Benjamin C.   African Religions: Symbol, Ritual and Community. New Jersey: Prentice Hall, 1976

Shorter, Aylward.	Religious Values in Kimbu Historical Charters. Africa 34, (1969)
Vansina, J.	Oral Tradition and History. London. James Currey . 1985.
Verner, A.	Myths and Legends of the Bantu. 1925. Reissued in 1968.
Westcott. J.A.	The Scripture and Myth of Eshu-Elegba. The Yoruba Trickster. Africa 32 (1962) pp 336 – 354.

·

www.ingramcontent.com/pod-product-compliance
Lightning Source LLC
Chambersburg PA
CBHW020245290326
41930CB00038B/356